METAVERSE

INVESTING

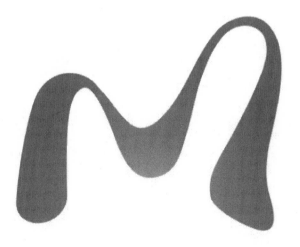

The Meta-Verse

ABOUT THE AUTHOR

The Meta-Verse

The Meta-Verse are technology researchers

Based in London, England.

The Meta-Verse is a collective; we work with the most senior academic researchers.

We are in the changing lives business.

Want Free Goodies?

Email us at:

mindsetmastership@gmail.com

Find us on Instagram!

@MindsetMastership

MASTERSHIP BOOKS

UK | USA | Canada | Ireland | Australia

India | New Zealand | South Africa | China

Mastership Books is part of the United Arts Publishing House group of companies based in London, England, UK.

First published by Mastership Books (London, UK), 2021

I S B N: 9 7 8 1 9 1 5 0 0 2 0 6 8

Cover design by Rich © United Arts Publishing (UK)

Text and internal design by Rich © United Arts Publishing (UK)

Image credits reserved.

Colour separation by Spitting Image Design Studio

Printed and bound in Great Britain

National Publications Association of Britain

London, England, United Kingdom.

Paper design UAP

ISBN: 9781-91500-2068 (paperback)

A723.5

Title: Metaverse Investing

Design, Bound & Printed:

London, England,

Great Britain.

METAVERSE

BEGINNERS GUIDE TO INVESTING

CONTENTS

0

INTRODUCTION

History of the Metaverse

Simulation is not merely a reflection of ourselves in the mirror. With technological advancement, we may observe creating a "growing network of persistent, real-time generated 3D worlds and simulations," currently referred to as "the metaverse." But where did this concept come from? What is the history of metaverse?

The word was originally used by author Neal Stephenson in his novel "Snow Crash" in 1992. The metaverse is a simulated landscape wherein people interact with avatars (initially a Hindu idea) and other computer programs. Real estate may be purchased and sold.

Hiro, the novel's central character, is a slum-dwelling pizza delivery guy and hacker. When he connects to the metaverse, his physical environments vanish. He was completely absorbed in this digital space. Hiro was respected in this virtual world because he had property. One can determine one's own identity while in this simulated condition. Everything is a fabrication. Within the sphere of a subjective becoming, identity formation might be carved into your portrayed character. The metaverse creates the tools to simulate our most cherished desires into digital society tokenization. As a result, one's metaverse identity is a phantom within a Neo Nation-State. You can dress up as a gorilla, a dragon, or a huge talking penis.

Academics, philosophers, and celebrities, in addition to Stephenson, have been skirting the edges of what is now widely acknowledged as a newly formed 'hyper reality' inside the metaverse. William Gibson's brief story "Burning Chrome," which was the first to describe the notion of "cyberspace," has hints of this. In his book "Neuromancer," Gibson expands on this previously virtual concept:

He described cyberspace as a collective delusion shared by billions of legal operators worldwide and youngsters learning mathematical principles. A graphic display of data extracted from the banks of all computers in the human system. Complexity beyond comprehension. Light lines spanned the nonspace of the mind, clusters, and data constellations.

Cyberspace is a vast network that links all forms of digital technology. Although cyberspace and the metaverse are not synonymous, they both live in the same world of possibility. The "Matrix" movie, production of Wachowskis and Joel Silver, was influenced by earlier movies such as "Dark City," "Lawnmower Man," "Total Recall," and the anime "Ghost in the Shell." On the other hand, the movie's concept may be dated directly to Jean Baudrillard, a French theorist. The Wachowskis' thinking was so influenced by Baudrillard's work that "Simulacra" is frequently seen as a prop on set during the first film.

The Wachowskis' line of thought may be traced back to Plato's renowned Allegory of the Cave. The arms and necks of a group of captives were chained together in this cave deep beneath. They could only see the shadows of puppets playing against the wall since it was so dark. All the captives knew were the shadows. They were completely unaware that their world was a computer simulation. One of the captives managed to break free from his chains and venture above ground one day. The brightness from above temporarily blinded him. He saw an entirely new world of color and clarity as his sight gradually adjusted. His perspective was abruptly transformed when he realized that all he had learned about the universe up to that point had been only a substitute for the actual thing.

The Evolution of Web1

Technological advancement is a continuous process. Nothing occurs in a day. Take, for example, the Industrial Revolution, which spanned the years 1760 to 1840. It began in the United Kingdom and spread across Europe and the United States. The introduction of automation via equipment was the focus of the Industrial Revolution. Everything was handcrafted before the start of this time. It was the Era of the Machine.

The evolution of the web itself may be regarded as a reflection of Web3 and its interaction with the metaverse. Web1 was the system that provided the basis for creating standards that would allow a device to send another set of instructions. Many computers may connect and follow these instructions simultaneously, allowing them to communicate with one another. This technique allows a computer to exchange a document or software with another, resulting in the Internet's foundation. The majority of web1 users were passive, unable to create their content unless they could create their websites.

The urge to achieve more with the internet than web1 permitted, such as showcasing user-produced content and online groups, led to web2 and commercial firms keen to fill the gaps. Big tech arose from the demand for more and more data and means to categorize and access it, resulting in Google's fast growth and the rise of social media such as Facebook. Individuals could perceive themselves as active users on the Internet and active players in the growth of its capabilities, thanks to the companies behind it hastened the reality of actualizing human wishes.

The disadvantage of this advancement is that these businesses have achieved efficiency and convenience by using private servers. This compares them to demi-gods that can gather and retrieve data while establishing their own set of laws and regulations. Anything uploaded or posted on their sites becomes their property instantly. They have complete control over the market and everything inside it.

Web3 makes use of blockchain's decentralized characteristics to create an ecosystem of anonymity. The person holds control and privacy over themselves and their possessions in this environment. Web3 establishes protocols with blockchain, establishing the basis for a new set of norms and activities. Blockchain transcends borders and aids in the development of a feeling of digital ownership and identity. It creates a level playing field. And in doing so, it establishes a foundation for what will come.

The phrase 'the metaverse' has been defined and reinterpreted several times. Although Stephenson is credited with establishing a framework for our knowledge of the metaverse, the concept is still developing. In the next section, we will talk about the meaning of the metaverse.

Meaning of Metaverse

There is no widely agreed-upon definition of a true metaverse other than a fancier version of the internet. Metaverse proponents, Silicon Valley, frequently quote Matthew Ball, a venture investor and author of the comprehensive Metaverse Primer:

Metaverse is a vast network of persistent, real-time generated 3D worlds and simulations that enable identity, objects, history, payments, and entitlements and can be experienced simultaneously by a practically infinite number of users, each with their feeling of presence.

Facebook, probably the largest tech corporation with a stake in the metaverse, puts it more succinctly:

Metaverse' is a collection of virtual locations where you can develop and explore with individuals who aren't physically there with you.

There are also more general metaverse categories, such as game designer Raph Koster, who distinguishes between online worlds, multiverses, and metaverses.

Online Worlds

According to Koster, online worlds are digital places centered on a single core subject, ranging from sophisticated 3D landscapes to text-based ones.

Multiverses, such as the OASIS in Ready Player One, are many distinct worlds linked in a network that do not have a single theme or rulebook.

On the other hand, a metaverse is a multiverse that interacts more with the actual world, including augmented reality overlays, virtual reality changing rooms in real stores, and even apps like Google Maps.

Transition of Companies

For example, at a Facebook Connect augmented and virtual reality conference in October 2021, Facebook announced that it had changed its name to Meta.

The name change reflects the company's expanding goals beyond social media. Facebook's new name, Meta, describes the company's ambition for working and playing in a virtual environment.

In addition to the name change, the firm announced that its stock symbol would change from FB to MVRS on December 1st. However, there will be no changes in how the social media application is used. Additionally, the name change will not affect the other social media platforms such as Instagram and Whatsapp.

A rebranding might be an effort to restore Facebook's reputation and turn the page after a string of public relations disasters, including disinformation on its platforms, content moderation breaches, and disclosures about its products' bad impact on some people' mental health.

Key Attributes of Metaverse

We identify six essential attributes of the metaverse:

- Identity

Participants may represent themselves as anyone or anything they choose with their avatar while virtually active in the metaverse. To paraphrase the science-fiction film Ready Player One, which describes the Oasis, an endless metaverse: "Individuals come to the Oasis for all the stuff they can do, but they remain for all the features they desire: tall, gorgeous, terrifying, a different sex, a different species, live-action, cartoon, anything you want to be."

- Multi-device access

The online virtual reality (VR) experience that employs a head-mounted device to immerse people in a computer-generated universe where they may control virtual items is expected to be one of the most significant advancements. The key characteristic is the ability to access the metaverse from whatever device, including the smartphone, computer, tablet, or other devices. Traditional displays and gadgets can also be used to access lighter versions of the metaverse.

- Immersive

A fully immersive feature involves using all five senses: sight, hearing, touch, smell, and taste. Presently, a virtual reality mostly consists of surrounding sound and visuals. Haptic body suits and omnidirectional treadmills might be among the future generation of virtual reality gadgets, providing participants with real sensations via electro-stimulation while they explore a digital landscape.

- Economy

A fully established metaverse feature has a working economy where participants may earn and spend digital or fiat currency. Roblox and its token, the Robux, are a typical example of a metaverse with a virtual economy. Robux may be spent on experiences and products for the avatar of those who buy it. Developers and producers may receive Robux by creating engaging experiences and appealing products that participants want to buy, converting their Robux to fiat currencies such as the US Dollar.

- Community

Using video games as an early precursor of the metaverse, we have observed that facilitating social experiences appears to be a key characteristic of successful titles. Participants are not in isolation in the metaverse; they are surrounded by people sharing experiences and engaging with one another in real-time. Compared to other gamers, Activision Blizzard CEO Rob Kotick stated that users who play in communities with colleagues and friends devote over three times more time to the game and about three times more on in-game content.

- Real-time Persistent

The metaverse is anticipated to be persistent in real-time, with no way to halt it. Even after participants have departed, it persists to exist and operate. This characteristic moves the participant's centricity to the virtual environment itself.

Popular Misconception

It's also useful to analyze what the metaverse is frequently compared to, albeit erroneously. Although these comparisons are most likely a component of the metaverse, they aren't the metaverse themselves. The metaverse, for instance, isn't.

- A virtual world

Virtual worlds and games featuring AI-supported characters, as well as those filled with "actual" individuals in real-time, have existed for years. This is an artificial and fictitious universe, not a metaverse with a single goal (a game).

- A virtual space

Digital content experiences such as Second Life are frequently referred to as "proto-metaverses" since they (A) lack game-like objectives or skill systems; (B) are persistent virtual hangouts; (C) provide near-synchronous content updates; (D) feature real people depicted by digital avatars. These, nevertheless, are insufficient characteristics for the metaverse.

- A virtual reality (VR)

VR is a method of immersing oneself in a virtual environment or place. A sense of presence in a digital environment isn't enough to constitute a metaverse. It's the same as claiming to live in a prosperous metropolis because you can see and walk about it.

- A digital and virtual economy

Individual games such as World of Warcraft have had a functional economy for a long time, where real individuals sell virtual items for real money or do digital jobs for real money. Furthermore, platforms like Amazon's Mechanical Turk and technology like Bitcoin are built on the employment of individuals/businesses/computing power to execute virtual and digital jobs. We are already trading at scale for completely digital products for completely digital activities through completely digital markets.

- A game

Fortnite is a "game" with numerous metaverse components. It:

- Mashes together IP(B)
- Has a consistent identity that covers several closed platforms
- Is a portal to a diverse range of experiences, many of which are merely social
- Pays content producers, among other things.

Nevertheless, like with Ready Player One, it is still too limited in what it can accomplish, how far it can go, and what "work" can be done. While the metaverse may have certain game-like aims, contain games, and use gamification, it is not a game in and of itself, nor is it focused on certain goals.

- A virtual Disneyland or theme park

Not only will there be an unlimited number of "attractions," but they will also not be "planned" or "coded" in the same way that Disneyland is, nor will they all be about pleasure or entertainment. Furthermore, the interaction distribution will have a very long tail.

- A new app store

Nobody needs a new method to launch applications, and doing so "in virtual reality" (for instance) would not unlock/enable the kinds of value promised by a successor Internet. The metaverse differs significantly from today's Internet/mobile design, paradigms, and goals.

- A new UGC platform

The metaverse will be a location where true empires are formed. The metaverse isn't just another YouTube or Facebook-like network where numerous people may "produce," "share," and "monetize" content, with the most famous content accounting for only a small portion of total consumption. Like with the web, a dozen or more platforms are likely to control a substantial portion of user time, experiences, content, and so on.

The Catalyst of the Metaverse Adoption

It is not a question of whether, but when we will see widespread metaverse activity. A variety of factors are speeding up our move to the virtual environment.

- Consumer Behavior

Consumer trends are an early signal for companies to sit up and take notice, and we are experiencing a lot of momentum when it comes to virtual behavior acceptance.

This transition is being driven in part by Generation Z. Gaming platforms are firstly a social environment for this class. Hanging out with pals in virtual environments has gone mainstream, and the attraction is increasingly reaching out to people of all ages.

People are becoming increasingly interested in interactive technology and want to understand more about it. Over half of those polled by Neilsen recently expressed a desire to use virtual reality and augmented reality more in their daily lives. With 73 percent of customers saying they would love to explore a brand's virtual home, it appears we have arrived at the right time to investigate how this sort of interactive experience may play out in the metaverse.

- Digital Fashion

Spending more time in virtual environments coincides with another emerging new craze: the digital fashion industry.

People may try to augment their real-life style — the ultimate representation of individualism — with digital fashion and cryptocurrency clothes. By the end of 2022, annual expenditure on gaming loot boxes and avatar skins is expected to reach a stunning $50 billion.

Furthermore, the economic and environmental advantages of digital shopping over physical shopping are crucial to the eco-friendly movement, making digital shopping in the metaverse an enticing and promising option.

- NFTs

The year 2021 will be remembered as a watershed moment for nonfungible tokens. In just three months, the market rose by an incredible 1785 percent, indicating their increasing popularity. This spike in nonfungible token usage increases the value of digital assets, which is piquing interest in the virtual economy.

The concept of a new trend for digital consumption increased so does the concept of an alternate universe to find, accumulate, and engage with these products grows more common.

- Wearables

While we are not yet at Ready Player One level, the much-anticipated release of extended reality wearables on the consumer market is edging closer. There is every possibility that this will complete the transition to universal metaverse adoption.

Wearables will provide you access to virtual business environments 24/7, no matter where you are. Whether you are alone at home, out shopping, or out having fun with friends, you will be able to enjoy a variety of unique brand experiences with just a tap.

Apple, Facebook, Google, and Snapchat have all put their names in the hat in the big wearable race. The massive investment from these technology behemoths will cause the most significant market disruption ever.

Advantages of Business-owned Metaverse

For future-oriented businesses, metaverse development is the most creative and commercially viable option. Let us have a look at why this is so:

- Meta-versatility

Being able to respond to changing needs and modify things up as much as possible without consulting the system is a huge advantage for businesses. Do you need to keep up with the most recent product lines? Simple. Do you want to establish any unique breakout areas? Make it happen.

Businesses may customize their content and environments anyway they want, thanks to this flexibility. They can build bizarre, otherworldly landscapes that can be continuously improved, altered, or even fully recreated in a short amount of time.

Businesses can seamlessly keep up with the speed of culture while maintaining complete creative control by becoming owners of their world.

- Keep it on-brand

Controlling content also implies that the digital environment as a whole can be kept on-brand. Although metaverse participants may have to meet the standard set by Roblox or Fortnite, metaverse builders may define their limits and have complete control over how their business is viewed, from layout to visuals to activities and messages.

This enables virtual users to fully submerge themselves in the brand without the possibility of compromise from third-party platforms.

- All under one virtual umbrella

The most significant advantage is that owned metaverses enable all business operations to be centralized in one location. Different applications for every new campaign, ephemeral microsites for unique items, and online events for different time zones are no longer necessary. Everything can exist together in a readily accessible area for participants worldwide to engage and enjoy 24/7 with a virtual brand world.

Because everything is enclosed, there is only one path to buy, making it easier than ever for metaverse participants to meet, communicate, play, explore, and make purchases – all in one location.

- Expand your tribe

A brand metaverse could achieve the same result in the virtual realm as a purpose-driven physical flagship can do in the physical environment, with one important distinction: the reach will be far greater than in a physical world context.

This implies that companies may grow and build their global audience by giving people an endless shared place to communicate with one another and the company while discussing their hobbies and interests. The power of a unified tribe behind a business cannot be overstated, and growing and nurturing these links would be a wise strategic option for any commercially focused business.

The Principles of Creating Virtual World

The advantages are apparent, but businesses must keep several crucial concepts in mind to build the most powerful and interactive metaverse experiences that will keep virtual users returning for more.

- Design unimaginable world

Don't simply design, reimagine. When it comes to creating an event or an experience, you have total creative freedom to create wholly unique and fantastical worlds.

Technology enables us to do the unthinkable – this is an opportunity to completely reimagine a setting rather than simply reproduce it and provide your audience with something unique that they would never be able to imagine in real life. Real-time audience participation, experimenting with dimensions, and displaying hypnotic images may all be used to improve the virtual world and create a really fantastic, unimaginable experience.

@Natalie

- Do not neglect emotion

Give your viewers the warm and fuzzies. The power to elicit emotion is at the heart of any effective experience, virtual or physical.

It is critical to generate compelling content that excites users and elicits an emotional response. Consider, for instance, a virtual concert. It is crucial to replicate the mutual flow of energy between stage performance and the crowd, which is achievable owing to immersive sound and stunning visual effects. An interactive metaverse experience needs to stir up these human emotions, producing an environment that makes a lasting effect on the users, much as a rush of adrenaline to the brain when you are among an agitated crowd.

- Participation

Put the consumer in charge. Getting hands-on with a business is one of the most compelling brand experiences, and virtual environments should be no different. The audience is transformed into a user when they take an active role, which assures long-term influence.

Brand lovers are expressing an increasing demand for decentralization in a world where anybody can now be a creator. This can be facilitated by virtual worlds that provide real-time, AI-driven, or customized interactions that enable participants to control events in their world. We may allow audiences to influence events within a virtual business environment via interactive streams, aggregated comments, and click control – whether it be activating VFX, initiating audio, or even leaving their footprint on the environment.

- Create scarcity

This drives supply and demand. Even though metaverse removes capacity limits and enables large masses to be reached, there are benefits to keeping particular activations limited to develop a feeling of uniqueness for visitors who are the "only ones" who enjoy that specific experience.

In the physical world, scarcity will always correspond to perceived worth. This impact must be produced in the virtual space – by restricting sign-ups, scheduling viewing times, or utilizing a blockchain system and ultimately boosting demand.

- Continue to evolve

Keep the relationship going. Businesses may not only own the design and customize the construction, but they can also collect data to monitor interaction and fine-tune the whole experience by creating their metaverses. The greatest virtual brand environments will use these data to create fresh, inventive, and dynamic content to keep consumers interested and returning for more.

The complexity of traversing multi-platform, virtual user experiences will also be seen as the new CX frontier by intuitive businesses, who will adjust to purchase funnels that span both virtual and physical worlds to improve the experience even more.

Metaverse Potentials

Even though the metaverse comes short of science fiction authors' fanciful dreams, it is expected to generate trillions of dollars in worth as a novel computer platform or content medium. However, in its complete form, the metaverse serves as a portal to most digital experiences and an essential piece of all physical ones and the next major labor network.

The benefit of being a significant player, if not a driver, in such a network is self-evident. Still, virtually all of the biggest online businesses are among the world's top ten most profitable public companies. And, if the metaverse truly serves as a viable "successor" to the web, with much more reach, time spent, and economic activity, there will certainly be even more economic benefits. Nevertheless, the Metaverse should provide the same breadth of potential as the web — new firms, products, and services will arise to handle everything from payment systems to identity verification, employment, ad distribution, content development, and security, among other things. As a result, several incumbents are expected to lose their seats.

The metaverse, in general, has the potential to change how we distribute and commercialize modern resources. For millennia, industrialized economies have changed as labor, and real estate scarcity grew and fell. Would-be workers living outside of urban centers will engage in the "high value" economy through digital labor in the metaverse. We'll see more adjustments in where we live, the constructed architecture, and who do particular activities as more consumer purchases switch to virtual products, services, and experiences. Consider the concept of "Gold Farming." Many "players" – often hired by a bigger firm and generally from lower-income nations – would devote a workday accumulating digital items for sale inside or outside the game not long after in-game trade economies began. In the West, these sales were generally to higher-income players. While most "labor" is tedious, repetitive, and restricted to a few uses, the variety and worth of this "work" will expand in tandem with the metaverse.

Metaverse Tech Stack

Components of Metaverse

Now is the time to figure out the most crucial features to include in a blockchain metaverse. Most importantly, the metaverse should be a totally open landscape rather than governed by a single entity. There are different components of the metaverse. The following elements, on the other hand, constitute the essential component of the metaverse.

Internet

As a decentralized network of devices, the internet is an important part of the metaverse. It is not controlled by any single institution, individual, or country. It makes no mention of the necessity for such entities' usage to be approved by a central authority.

Standards for Open Media

The blockchain metaverse can achieve real interoperability only by providing open standards for media like music, text, and video. The development of media and its effort to create new kinds of media must be governed by the standards. Pixar's USD and NVIDIA's MDL are important moves toward strengthening open media standards for 3D applications and facilitating interoperability.

Open Programming Languages Standards

The metaverse also requires a plethora of open and transparent programming language standards. These standards will regulate the usage of various programming languages in the metaverse to create apps. Consequently, script compatibility between languages like HTML, Shader Language, WebAssembly, WebGPU, JavaScript, and WebXR is possible.

Extended Reality (XR) Hardware

The extended reality or XR hardware is also a key component in responses to the question "what is a blockchain metaverse?" The goal of XR hardware is to create a connection between the actual world and the metaverse. Omni treadmills, smart glasses, and haptics are just a few examples of XR hardware in the metaverse.

Smart Contracts and Decentralized Ledger

Decentralized ledgers and smart contract networks would clearly be the ultimate element to the architecture of a blockchain metaverse. Blockchain networks are required to provide transaction transparency and censorship resistance. Similarly, the blockchain network would ensure that no transactions require authorization.

Ethereum, Theta, Bitcoin, Binance Smart Chain (BSC), and Flow are a few popular blockchain systems utilized in the metaverse. Consequently, it can provide a solid foundation for the ownership economy, enabling the metaverse to grow.

1

VIRTUAL REALITY

Meaning of Virtual Reality (VR)

Virtual reality, or VR, enables individuals to be immersed in a simulated world. This is generally (but not always) accomplished by using head-mounted hardware that records an individual's motions. A screen (or two display panels, one for each eye) is enclosed in a frame (or headset) that is fastened or attached to your head. A pair of lenses is generally attached between the panels and your eyes, shutting off the outside world to make it look like what you see via the headset is your whole environment.

Importantly, all headsets monitor your movement and modify the picture you see appropriately. Some headsets, on the other hand, monitor movement more than others. Virtual reality experiences usually provide a way for you to manipulate or select items inside the simulated world. In certain cases, you'll have a controller in each hand to control different parts of the game. In certain situations, the controllers provide virtual depictions of your hands that may be used to influence the environment and items inside it in ways that are comparable to those found in the real world.

Basic Terminology and Concepts

So you've grasped the fundamentals of virtual reality, but there are a few terminology or ideas that need to be clarified.

FOV (Field of View)

FOV is an abbreviation for the phrase "field of view." In the context of the eyes, our field of view refers to all we can see at any point in time.

The field of view represents all you can see in the digital world at any point in time when wearing a VR headset. The virtual reality headsets have a field of view that is less than what you can see with your eyes, which means the virtual reality world does not fill, or equal, your eyes' field of view whenever you use the VR headset.

When utilizing a VR headset, you'll see a black "border" surrounding the lenses you're viewing through. This is merely the area surrounding the lenses on the inside of the VR headset. However, if the headset's field of view is sufficiently wide, the boundary may make it appear as if you're staring through a pair of glasses into the virtual environment. This makes it possible to forget about the limit. FOV is assessed in various ways, and device makers may not correctly describe how much you can see compared to other headsets.

Degrees of Freedom

Individuals commonly refer to "degrees of freedom," or DoF, when discussing movement and monitoring in virtual reality. More DoF means the VR headset will track and transfer more of your bodily movements onto your virtual simulation.

When it comes to DoF, the two most prevalent words you'll come across are 3DoF and 6DoF. (3 and 6 degrees of freedom, respectively). Only 3DoF VR headsets capture your head's motions (roll, pitch, and yaw), but not its location in space (x, y, z plane). 6DoF can track your head's motions as well as its coordinates in space.

The majority of virtual reality headsets now have complete 6DoF positional tracking. Most older mobile and standalone VR headsets, like Google Cardboard, Google Daydream, Gear VR, and Oculus Go, employ 3DoF.

Tracking Types

Every virtual reality headset must be able to track the movement of the user. "Inside Out" track is now the most popular method of tracking. This technology usually uses cameras integrated within the virtual reality headset to detect movement from the inside outwards. Advanced "SLAM" (simultaneous location and mapping) systems detect elements of the real world around the individual using the headset. Inside-out tracking is used by the Oculus Quest, Oculus Rift S, HTC Vive Cosmos, and all Windows Mixed Reality headsets (such as the Samsung Odyssey, Lenovo Explorer, Acer HMD, and others).

There's again "Outside-in" tracking. This could take many different shapes, but it always entails hardware that is not integrated into the VR headset and is external to the tracked region. This hardware is frequently referred to as "lighthouses" about the original HTC Vive and Valve Index, which are little black boxes installed in the corners of the room. Older systems, such as the 2016 Rift, employed customized cameras in the room to perform outside tracking.

All tracking method has their own set of advantages and disadvantages. Without the need for setup or mounting hardware, inside-out tracking may be used more readily. On the other hand, outside-in tracking may be extended to fill gaps where head-mounted hardware may be unable to "notice" infrequent body movements. In tracking movements, common solutions require a direct line of sight to "see" whatever they are tracking. Since our bodies move in diverse ways, both inside out and outside in tracking methods might be obstructed in numerous ways. Nevertheless, based on the application, an inside out or outside in system may be more appropriate.

Controllers

Engaging with virtual content may be done in several ways. Headsets such as the Oculus Quest 2, HP Reverb G2, and HTC Vive Cosmos generally have two controllers, one per hand, and the inside-out tracking technology tracks them in 6 degrees of freedom.

Various input methods are available in PlayStation virtual reality. Using a pair of PlayStation Move controllers is usually the best choice. The Move controllers are required for certain PSVR content, though not all. You may use the regular PS4 DualShock controller with games that don't need Move controllers.

The Valve Index Controllers include a strap that wraps across your knuckles and palm and allows for a complete release. The controllers have a big grip area and can track all hand movements and some of the pressure supplied by your grip, which sets them apart from other controllers. External lighthouses monitor these controllers, which may be purchased with the Index VR headset. They may equally be bought separately and used in conjunction with non-Index VR headsets that employ the lighthouse tracking technology, like the HTC Vive or Pimax.

Roomscale, Seated, and Standing

Roomscale, seated, and standing are the three most common forms of tracked volumes with software suited to each play area size.

Setting a border or play area in roomscale virtual reality is all about easily and physically walking about that region in the game. The concept behind roomscale games is that you may physically walk around your space and connect with the virtual space and things inside it. So-called "guardian" or "chaperone" barriers appear to show when the physical space approaches.

Seated and standing are comparable in that the participant is supposed to stay in about the same location and utilize various movement choices to mimic movement rather than moving psychically across space. Many software developers create virtual environments that may be used differently, although a tiny percentage of them may only operate in roomscale, seated, or standing modes.

Movement in Virtual Reality

For virtual reality software, there are several distinct sorts of simulated movement choices. VR headset users may experience nausea when simulating movement.

Teleporting is a frequent mode of transportation that is typically the most pleasant for many people. Teleport is usually triggered by pressing a button on a controller, after which the player picks a location to which they can teleport instantaneously. This mobility option, when combined with roomscale tracking, often enables easy traversal of vast simulated volumes. Nevertheless, some people claim that teleport is less convincing and "breaks immersion" as we can't teleport in the actual world. As a result, some virtual reality software creators explain why teleportation is a part of their virtual reality story.

Smooth locomotion is a kind of movement comparable to that of classic video games, in which you click a button and "move" in the direction you pushed the button. This might be startling for some individuals, making them feel sick in seconds or minutes.

Software engineers continuously strive to create combinations of current systems or comfort settings that enable users to customize their virtual reality experience to their taste to mitigate the discomfort caused by simulated movement in a virtual environment. One typical comfort option for reducing discomfort is limiting the field of view into the virtual environment while moving, resulting in a kind of "tunnel vision," or gradually increasing and reducing acceleration while traveling.

Motion Sickness

Wearing a virtual reality headset might be uncomfortable at times. You can develop nausea or motion sickness. Having nausea while wearing a

VR headset can often occur in sitting or standing situations where the game's movement does not match your actual body movement.

Many people can develop resistance and greater tolerance level for more intense experiences — this is sometimes referred to as "finding your virtual reality legs" — but many developers and early virtual reality enthusiasts who have spent hundreds of hours in virtual reality headsets are still completely vulnerable to irritation due to the disparity between seamless locomotion and their body's senses.

The FOV of the images, the frame rate of the screen and system, headset weight, and how well you slept or what you consumed and how much you consumed may all impact your sensitivity to irritation in the virtual reality headset.

IPD

 When studying and learning about virtual reality headsets, you'll stumble on the term "IPD." It refers to "interpupillary distance," which is defined as the distance between the centers of your two pupils.

Variable IPDs across persons might impact how good some headsets feel when used, based on the optical design of the VR headset. Images may look fuzzy if the lenses and screens in front of a person's pupil are not perfectly aligned. In the worst-case scenario, this might raise your chances of developing a headache or nausea.

A manual adjustment for IPD will be available on some headsets. The lenses and display panels are moved closer to the pupils of a wide variety of individuals due to this. Other VR headsets may not enable you to change manually, but they may provide a software adjustment to accommodate individual differences.

A VR headset with manual adjustment may be required based on the distance separating your pupils. Most individuals may not require a headset with manual adjustment since headsets without manual adjustments are frequently suited to the usual distances between eyes.

Types of Virtual Reality

There are different types of virtual reality equipment on the market. These are divided into three categories: standalone VR, PC VR, and console VR.

Standalone VR

Any VR headset that functions fully independently of any other equipment or technology is a standalone VR. The whole experience is controlled by the headset you wear on your head and does not need any other devices.

The finest example is Oculus Quest 2, which provides stripped-down versions of PC VR games in a compact and independent device that doesn't need additional hardware. Everything you require to enjoy virtual reality comes with standalone VR like the Quest. However, certain games require you to hold the Oculus Touch controllers in your hands to participate.

PC VR

Any VR that needs a continuous connection to a close PC is referred to as PC VR. The PC in question will, at the same time, need to have sufficient specifications to support VR. The Oculus Rift S, Valve Index, HTC Vive, Pimax, and Windows Mixed Reality headsets such as the HP Reverb G2 and Samsung Odyssey+ are just a few examples of PC VR headsets.

The benefit of PC VR is that it can give considerably greater graphics quality than standalone VR due to the hefty PC specifications. Several wireless PC VR alternatives usually need additional hardware linked to the PC and a battery pack carried somewhere on the body. In wired PC VR, you must handle a cord that connects the headset to the computer. The cord can be a constant reminder that you can get tangled when you spin around too much. Thus it may give less flexibility than a wireless solo headphone.

PC VR may rapidly become a costly alternative if you don't already have a gaming PC that fulfills the minimum specifications.

Console VR

For the Nintendo Switch, there are just two virtual reality headsets available: PlayStation VR and Nintendo Labo VR.

PlayStation VR is a PS4 or PS5 VR add-on system. The PSVR headset is an add-on that attaches to the PS4 and, like PC VR, needs a continual tethered connection to the system to work. It tracks with the PS camera, which comes with the headset and is linked to the system. The system equally works on PS5 thanks to backward compatibility, with minor aesthetic and performance enhancements. To enjoy some PS VR games, you'll need to buy PlayStation Move controllers separately.

Nintendo Labo VR for the Nintendo Switch is a cardboard VR headset shell built and inserted into the original full-size Nintendo Switch, enabling you to play selected games in virtual reality. Because there is no VR headset strap, you must keep the headset to the face. Most of the Labo VR experiences are, to put it bluntly, disappointing and not worthy of your time.

Major Players

Oculus VR

In 2016, Facebook paid a staggering $2 billion for the firm. John Carmack, the creator of id Software's 'Doom,' was also part of the team. Carmack later departed Oculus due to legal conflicts with ZeniMax, but the company's creative engines have not slowed down.

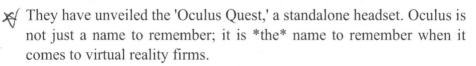 They have unveiled the 'Oculus Quest,' a standalone headset. Oculus is not just a name to remember; it is *the* name to remember when it comes to virtual reality firms.

Google

Yes, Google is among the major players in the virtual reality space. Gone are the days of searching for things like "how to tie a tie" and "pie recipes." Google is currently experimenting with virtual reality. It was a fantastic move for them to appear on the scene. They unveiled the 'Google Cardboard,' a $15 cardboard virtual reality headset.

It was created to be worn over your phone or device and engage with various apps and games. It is easy to imagine Google continuing to investigate the field of virtual reality and even branching out with a greater presence.

HTC Vive

The HTC Vive is a hybrid of The Matrix, Ready Player One, and the cyberpunk genre. This headset was introduced by HTC for $799, distinguishing experts from beginners. It comes with a headset, room sensors, and portable gadgets. One of the things to admire about HTC is that they collaborated on this initiative with Valve to make it more powerful.

This, I am sure, applies to a lot of VR Steam games. They received such a good mark not just because of the technology they provide but also because this VR business is teaming up with a firm to change the VR sector with tanklesslab.

You will be walking around the area with their headset, not just sitting in a lonely spot.

Unity

Unity is a well-known developer in the area of 3D animation. Therefore, it is no coincidence that they have produced VR-ready software. Most interesting virtual reality content has gone through the Unity 3D engine, making Unity an important VR and a leading VR firm.

One look at their site reveals an outstanding portfolio of achievements and content to use in your creative efforts.

Microsoft

Microsoft is another famous name and another potential virtual reality heavy hitter. Microsoft joins the list, demonstrating that virtual reality companies can be large, established businesses. Microsoft is putting a lot of emphasis on not only VR but also AR. The HoloLens is now available from Microsoft, and it enables not just games but also real applications.

Samsung

Many of the names we are familiar with from our daily lives appear here. They do so because, fortunately for them, they already have a technological head start, and Samsung is no newcomer to technology, including virtual reality. Samsung made a good move by collaborating with Oculus to create the Samsung hardware, a virtual reality headset.

It is more affordable, making it a more appealing choice for casual users. It is a VR headset for your smartphone, and you just slip the smartphone into the headset. Samsung has a lot of promise in this area, and I believe they can even start making games for their projects.

Magic Leap

Magic Leap is a startup business that is a shift from the list of virtual reality companies. Magic Leap is concentrating on augmented reality rather than complete virtual reality. They employ 3D elements to populate the scene surrounding the user, which I find fascinating. This offers the possibility of future development since they may become the market leader in augmented reality.

Magic Leap is marketing its 'Magic Leap One' with the phrase 'Free Your Mind.' They are just selling the creator version of the VR, so hopefully, the applications and games it uses will be completely functional by the time it hits the market.

WorldViz

WorldViz mostly creates virtual reality programs for schools. They also provide programs for architectural and safety training. Consider how beneficial it will be for architects to explore the many models they create rather than relying just on drawings and models. It would alter the way buildings are constructed, which is why more firms like WorldViz are needed.

Snap Inc.

Snap is the business that created Snapchat, so you know these folks are on top of their game in terms of technology. They are experts at incorporating AR into their technology, demonstrating that they can be a top VR firm. Every day, you may use your phone camera to explore different parts of A for free.

You may use 3D models to enhance pictures or videos of yourself or pals. This technology is making its way into the public without requiring hundreds of thousands in development and release.

Wevr

Wevr is largely driven by user-generated content. This technology is placed in the hands of ordinary people, which is quite appealing. With their initiative, they plan to make a mainstream virtual reality, the "YouTube of VR." Users will upload their content for people to enjoy in VR, making the process simple and smooth.

Firsthand Technology

This firm is promising due to its mission. It is a noble cause that VR firms should prioritize. They are mostly concerned with healthcare. The programs assist individuals who suffer from anxiety in reducing their symptoms. Imagine you have had a particularly stressful day, and your nerves are frayed. You put on your VR headset and begin to relax.

Because their product is dependent on heart rate, they advise consumers to relax while using it. This passes a significant threshold in VR; the company and product genuinely care about the user.

NextVR

NextVR is the virtual reality company for sports enthusiasts out there. It broadcasts sporting events, allowing you to feel closer to your desired sport.

Imagine being able to feel like you are at a Philadelphia Eagles game, such as their recent Super Bowl triumph against the New England Patriots, without having to pay the exorbitant ticket fees.

Nvidia

We are all familiar with Nvidia's legendary commitment to producing top-of-the-line graphics cards that allow you to enjoy your favorite games in the highest possible resolution. Nvidia, like Unity, provides virtual reality technology for creators and other virtual reality firms to employ to develop better apps and games.

They enable a clearer and fluid resolution when a participant or user is in the program or application, resulting in a more realistic experience for all parties involved.

Prenav

Drones, like virtual reality, have become a fixture in technology. Prenav provides drones with more sophisticated software to explore structures better than basic Google Maps or other GPS technologies. These drones keep the cell service working efficiently by building 3D models of mobile phone towers for drone inspection.

The significance of everything functioning is the primary reason for their high ranking on the best VR businesses list.

Osterhout Design Group

Osterhout brings the Watch Dogs gaming series to life for individuals who have played it. Their headset—or, more precisely, their glasses—provides you with useful information about what you are looking at. In comparison to Google Glass, Osterhout's technology may provide you with biographies of persons you are looking at, as well as other valuable features.

Imagine receiving a piece of furniture and being completely baffled as to how to put it together correctly. Osterhout assists you in putting it all together, removing the difficulties that come with some elements of daily living. That is such an essential objective for a VR firm.

Application of VR Outside Gaming

Virtual Reality in the Military

Both the British and American militaries have used virtual reality in their training because it allows them to do a wide range of impersonations. VR is used by all military departments, including the navy, army, air force, marines, and coast guard. VR may efficiently transfer a learner into some different scenarios, places, and surroundings to facilitate teaching.

Military applications include aviation, vehicle, warfare simulations, medic training, and creating a virtual boot camp. The technology provides a completely engaging experience with sights and music that can safely replicate dangerous training exercises for preparing and training soldiers while preventing exposure to danger until they are battle-ready. Additionally, while on the battlefield, the technology may educate soldiers in interacting with residents or foreign journalists.

Another use of virtual reality is for treating Post-Traumatic Stress Disorder (PTSD), which troops returning from battle frequently experience. They require aid in readjusting to civilian life.

Virtual Reality in Education

In addition to teaching and learning situations, virtual reality is being used in the education industry. It enables students to converse with one another in a 3D space. Students could also go on virtual field trips to art galleries, take solar system tours, and go back through time to other eras.

VR can be particularly beneficial for kids with special needs. According to research, virtual reality might be a compelling platform for properly training and teaching social skills to children with autistic problems. For example, Floreo, a technology firm, created VR scenarios that allow kids to acquire and practice eye contact, pointing, and forming social relationships.

Virtual Reality in Sports

VR has been slowly reshaping the sports business for all of its players. Coaches and athletes may use this technology to successfully train across a variety of sports since they will be able to watch and experience certain scenarios again, improving their performance each time.

Virtual reality is now being used as a training tool to assist in evaluating sports performance and skill. It has also been shown to help wounded players improve their mental skills by enabling them to experience game conditions digitally.

Similarly, the technology is being used to enhance the viewer's experience when viewing a sporting event. Many broadcasters have begun live streaming using VR. They are planning to offer virtual tickets for live sporting events, allowing fans from all around the world to attend any sporting event. This also allows individuals who cannot afford to spend money to attend live sporting events and feel involved since they can have a comparable experience from the comfort of their own homes, at no cost or a lower cost.

Virtual Reality in Mental Health

Virtual reality technology is being used to treat PTSD. An individual is immersed in a simulation of a traumatic experience using VRTD (Virtual Reality Exposure Therapy) to help the individual overcome the situation and begin to recover.

It is also used to treat emotions like anxiety, sadness, and phobias. Several individuals with anxiety, for example, have identified meditation using virtual reality as a beneficial way to handle stress sensitivity and improve coping skills. Virtual reality technology can provide a safe atmosphere for patients to confront the things they are afraid of while being protected and secure.

Virtual Reality in the Fashion Industry

One area of virtual reality's use case in the fashion business that has received far less attention is its use in the fashion industry. Virtual simulations of shop settings, for example, may be a very efficient way for merchants to practice building their signage and product exhibits without having to commit to the actual build.

Similarly, adequate efforts and money may be allocated to creating a shop layout. Tommy Hilfiger, Coach, and Gap are just a few of the well-known businesses that have begun to incorporate virtual reality into their operations. These companies are using virtual reality to provide customers a 360-degree view of fashion events and allow them to try on items virtually. ~ C's galleries

2

AUGMENTED REALITY

Meaning of Augmented Reality

According to Wikipedia, Augmented Reality (AR) is an immersive experience of the real-world situation in which things in the real world are augmented with computer-generated perceptual information. The Cambridge Dictionary defines AR as computer-generated visuals combined with a view of the actual world.

The first game that springs to mind when we think about Augmented Reality is Pokémon Go. AR, on the other hand, is not just for gamers. It is increasingly affecting the way businesses function and make choices. According to Goldman Sachs, the market for AR and VR technology would be worth $85 billion by 2025. Gaming and videos are at the center of most discussions about Augmented Reality. However, the non-entertainment usage of AR technology is driving a large market value.

Sutherland began his quest with Augmented Reality in 1968. AR, which began with a construction app, has grown to a new level. AR (Augmented Reality) is a system that allows users to connect with the real-world environment. AR uses computer-generated perceptual information to improve real-world items.

AR has three main characteristics:

- A mixture of the physical and virtual worlds
- A real-time interaction
- An exact representation of the actual and virtual item

AR is a technology that enhances reality to create something larger and better. AR technology allows users to have a fully interactive experience with the actual environment. Computer-generated reality and Mixed Reality are two often used synonyms for AR. Augmented reality is a seamless and comfortable technology that requires little instruction after being deployed in a certain field. In 2017, there were only 336 AR businesses listed on Angel List. By the year 2020, this number has risen to about 1 billion!

Evolution of AR

AR's evolution may be broken down into three distinct stages:

Attention stage

Ivan Sutherland, a computer scientist, invented the first Augmented reality technology in 1968. He was also referred to as "Father of Graphics." Sutherland invented the first augmented reality (AR) head-mounted display.

In addition, the year saw the development of one of the first AR applications for commercial usage. The creation of AR applications was done for the aim of advertising. AR was utilized in advertising by Munich-based German agencies. They developed a printed commercial for BMW Mini. The same appeared on the screen when the automobile model was held in front of the camera.

In 2008, the first commercial augmented reality application was released. It was created for advertising reasons by Munich-based German firms. They created a printed magazine ad for a BMW Mini model that appeared on the screen when held in front of a computer's camera. Eventually, major corporations like Disney, National Geographic, and Coca-Cola began to use Augmented reality and Virtual reality technologies.

Augmented reality has been used for a variety of applications. For example, National Geographic used AR to depict ancient creatures walking around a showroom rather than in a cage!

Coca-Cola employed augmented reality to raise awareness of the melting ice's environmental impact. Individuals had only heard of melting ice until that point, but Augmented reality allowed them to experience it in a shopping mall. In terms of increasing environmental issues, the effect would have been doubled.

Disney employed augmented reality to display cartoon characters on a huge screen and have them talk to people. It would have been fascinating to see!

Trial stage

The second stage of Augmented reality development began when digital items were modeled. The products may connect with the physical world and move in real-time, thanks to the simulation.

In the 2010s, the product classes that used Augmented reality were jewelry and watches. Throughout this era, the usage of AR for product "try on" became widespread. Apple Watch also provided a virtual try-on for bringing its watch to life.

Usage stage

Augmented reality was being used in a wider number of sectors at this point in its development. AR has progressed to the point that it is now one of the most useful technology for exploring geographic, historical, cultural, and environmental elements.

In the past, Augmented reality was used to transport travelers. Evolution applications for the tourism sector were created during this stage of Augmented reality. For instance, the Museum of London's augmented reality application allows guests to feel and explore streets from 1000 years ago. The AR software also brings the artworks in the museum to life.

Likewise, museum applications allow visitors to learn more about great artworks by putting a description on their phone displays in real-time.

Types of Augmented Reality

Even though all Augmented reality devices have a few features in common, there are several types of AR, each of which is better suited to distinct applications. We will go through five different types of AR and some of their pros and shortcomings.

Marker-based AR

Marker-based, also known as image recognition AR, uses a trigger item as a prompt to show content. A QR code or even a cereal box may be used as a trigger. This form of augmented reality takes the lowest amount of processing power and is very simple to create, but it is less flexible than other AR types since it depends on certain triggers.

Markerless AR

The versatility of markerless AR is greater than that of marker-based augmented reality. Rather than using trigger items, this sort of augmented reality tracks the user's location and displays pertinent information using cameras, GPS, and accelerometer data. This set of inputs is referred to as Simultaneous Localization and Mapping, or SLAM. Most forms of AR accessible today employ SLAM f or markerless experiences.

Projection-based AR

As the name indicates, projection-based augmented reality projects digital pictures straight onto objects or surfaces in the user interface. You may project a working keyboard on the desk using projection-based augmented reality. This form of augmented reality eliminates the need for a screen or headset, allowing users to create dreamlike experiences for huge groups of people. While remarkable, projection-based augmented reality is not always the best solution for smaller-scale applications.

Outlining AR

It is also very self-explanatory. This type of augmented reality employs picture recognition to define borders and shapes rather than altering the full scene. It is most often employed to assist drivers in navigating the road in low-light situations and direct pilots to airfields. If the Titanic had set sail right now, they might have avoided the iceberg by using augmented reality. But then Leo and Kate's emotional performances would never have captivated us.

Superimposition based AR

This uses object recognition to partially or completely substitute an object in the user interface with a digital picture. A doctor, for instance, might utilize AR to overlay a digital x-ray over a portion of a patient's body when in a surgical operation.

Industries Reaping Augmented Reality

The market has already become more competitive as a result of massive technical developments. Companies are constantly looking for new and innovative methods to attract and engage their consumers.

What could be a better solution than augmented reality? AR quickly establishes itself as a game-changing technology that opens up possibilities that are impossible to attain with conventional technologies. This reality has been recognized by certain industries, which are currently utilizing AR to boost performance.

Healthcare

Consider the first operation performed by a novice surgeon. Anxiety and fear could be the dominant emotions at the time. The novice surgeons now have a helping hand in the form of AR applications. In surgery, AR applications provide a video platform with simulated hands which can be used on the patients. Skilled surgeons utilize the simulated hands to train the fresh ones irrespective of their geographical position.

Education

Not every student is a voracious reader. Most people desire to learn, yet they may not find it engaging. Augmented reality in education is a ground-breaking AR technology that has aided people and kids in learning and comprehending their environment. The British Museum employs augmented reality technology to assist kids and adults in interpreting their statues. This augmented reality software makes use of a Samsung tablet and provides a game that youngsters may play.

Application of Augmented Reality

AR is an advanced technology that aids businesses in enhancing consumer satisfaction. This section will concentrate on how AR may be used in the real world.

AR in Airport Navigation

Terminal 1, Terminal 2, Terminal. It is never simple to find your way around an airport. The Gatwick Airport passenger application was created utilizing augmented reality to help travelers navigate the airport. The software navigates travelers around the airport using over 2,000 Bluetooth beacons. This software might become one of the instruments for managing airport traffic flow.

AR in Manufacturing

Did you have any reservations about buying furniture? The color may be a mismatch with the walls. In the room, the furniture may appear tiny and large, as well as several other flaws. Customers will benefit from the Ikea Place app, which is an augmented reality software. The software uses ARKit technology that enables users to scan a space to purchase furniture. By adding things to a new digital world, you may simply create the room and choose the color of the furniture that matches.

AR in Cosmetic Store

What color gloss should I wear if this one does not match my skin tone? Questions that are often asked when purchasing cosmetics. Cosmetics are an expensive purchase, and making the incorrect selection may result in money being wasted. Sephora, a cosmetics firm, is aware of this problem among its clients. As a result, the firm employs augmented reality technology to allow customers to sample items in a realistic setting before purchasing them!

AR in Healthcare

AR can also save lives! Yes, you read that correctly. Are you assuming that Augmented Reality will take the place of medications and procedures? No, definitely. In healthcare, augmented reality applications will give real-time data that may be utilized for patient diagnosis, therapy, and operation planning.

AR in Games

The concept behind augmented reality games and applications like Pokémon Go and Snapchat is now obvious. Is there any augmented reality game that comes to mind? By 2023, the market for augmented reality games is anticipated to reach $284.93 billion. Other than Pokémon, there are a variety of games to choose from, like Zombies Run, Ghostbuster World, and Kings of Pool.

Education

AR has the potential to improve teaching and learning. By converting previously static data and photos into immersive experiences, augmented reality can change textbooks and schools. When you can use AR to dissect the strata of a volcano or plunge hundreds of miles into the Earth's crust, geology becomes a lot more interesting.

Even flashcards, one of the most basic study aids, may benefit from augmented reality. Augmented reality Flashcards Animal Alphabet is an application that uses augmented reality to assist young kids in learning the alphabet by bringing flashcards to life. When the duck from the "D is for a duck" card stands in front of you, the ABCs appear a lot easier and more enjoyable.

Sports and entertainment

Even the manner we purchase Super Bowl tickets is evolving thanks to AR technology. StubHub launched a feature on its smartphone application for Super Bowl LII that allows ticket purchasers to view a virtual 3D model of US Bank Stadium and the surrounding region. This was not the firm's first time experimenting with augmented reality. StubHub formerly provided a "virtual view," which enabled people to experience the view from their seats before purchasing a ticket. StubHub saw its engagement increase in a year after releasing that option.

Many sports leagues have also used AR to improve their viewers' watching experience. The MLB's famous "At Bat" application now includes augmented reality capabilities that will enable users to see actual stats on every player, ball speed and distance covered, and other data by just pointing their phone at the field.

Mixed Reality

Mixed reality is a cutting-edge technology that incorporates features of both augmented reality and virtual reality. While virtual reality and augmented reality have been around for decades, mixed reality only debuted in 1994, making it a millennial phenomenon.

The phrase was originally used in a study titled "A Taxonomy of Mixed Reality Visual Displays" by Paul Milgram and Fumio Kishino. The concept of a virtual continuum was proposed in the article, which was described as combining categories of objects shown in any specific display scenario. The physical worlds are displayed at one end of the continuum, and virtual worlds are shown at the other.

Hence, a mixed-reality world is one in which the physical world and virtual world items are shown simultaneously inside a single display. A space somewhere between the edges of the virtuality continuum. People frequently confuse mixed reality with virtual or augmented reality, but the key is that the two technologies work together to produce mixed reality.

Application of Mixed Reality

Because the mixed reality is novel, there are not many commercial use cases. Furthermore, the commercial applications that have been implemented are still in their infancy. The manufacturing and medical industries are two of the most well-known mixed reality.

Manufacturing Application

Mixed reality may be highly useful in architectural settings like putting machines in a factory. People can, for instance, hold a phone or tablet screen up to an area of the factory and move virtual models of the machine around the area.

This technology equally aids in employee education and training. Employees on the manufacturing floor, for instance, can use a headset to get active instructions on how to handle machines, connect with supervisors online, and go through training sessions in readiness for business activities.

Without the requirement for the physical presence of employees or machines, AR and VR provide the potential to decrease maintenance cycle times and provide more training options. This also aids employees in reskilling and upskilling faster, providing them the resources to handle issues with less interruption.

Medical Applications

Mixed reality is being utilized in the medical profession to assist trainees in practice procedures and offer great visualization of operating theatre data during surgery to help the surgeon remain focused on their work rather than glancing away at a screen.

Other business use cases have circulated across the enterprise, focusing on increasing virtual work collaboration and partnership. Microsoft, for instance, recently revealed that Holoportation, which enables users with mixed reality headsets to view and connect with colleagues as a full-size 3D hologram, is still in development.

On the other hand, these technologies are still in the early phases of development and have not yet been widely deployed or proven.

Mixed Reality Headsets

Mixed reality headgear is still in the early phases of development in the workplace, with additional devices, like Apple's sensor-incorporated head-mounted display, being developed for future launch.

Here are a few of the popular mixed reality headsets on the market right now:

Microsoft HoloLens

HoloLens 2 is the newly released Microsoft headset, and it has Qualcomm's Snapdragon 850 computing engine and a proprietary AI holographic coprocessor. HoloLens 2 includes a flip-up visor, a wide vertical FOD, and flexible hand and eye-tracking and is targeted at corporate customers, particularly first-line workers.

Magic Leap One

Magic Leap is a spatial computing device that comes in the form of linked eyewear with a Lightpack or an external processor operated by a portable touchpad. The headset begins at $2,295 and may be customized with prescription lenses.

RealWear HMT-1

RealWear HMT-1 is a durable headset built particularly for enterprise employees in the field and was named Best Headworn Device at the 10th annual Augmented World Expo. These gadgets give information to a task, like data and instructions for hands-free engineering and warehousing operations. The gadget is quite simple, with few bells and whistles, and it costs little under $1,500.

Oculus Quest

Facebook's Oculus Quest has been effectively utilized for workplace training, as Walmart has demonstrated, and its Oculus for Business software is extremely helpful for companies. This software package comprises device setup and administration tools, enterprise-grade service, and a unique user interface tailored to the specific needs of each organization.

Extended Reality

Extended Reality is abbreviated as XR. It is the next stage in interactive storytelling, data visualization, social networking, and more. Individuals all around the globe are turning to digital worlds and digital products to remain connected with their pals, family, and colleagues as a result of the COVID pandemic.

At least in the United States, the physical world will only provide limited interactions. This implies that digital environments and virtual products are functionally equivalent to their physical-world counterparts. This would have been an unimaginable technological advancement just a few years ago. It has now become mainstream in the world.

Pros and cons of Extended Reality

For today's world, XR promises a new terrain of exploration and creativity. The potential of extended reality will only expand when new technology in haptic technology and cognitive control develops. The following are some of the advantages and disadvantages to consider right now:

Pros

- Limitless creativity

Visualizing and playing with 3D representations of items and designs allows for far more innovation.

- Enhanced collaboration

Unlike traditional video or voice conferencing, XR may bring individuals together with a far more realistic sense of immersion.

- Improved learning

In practically all contexts, having access to contextual information, demonstrations, and 3D representations enable improved and greater learning experiences.

- Enhanced productivity and effectiveness

In an extended reality environment, workers can collaborate and work much more quickly and efficiently than they could if they were exchanging emails.

- New experiences

From digital events to holidays, extended reality technologies allow us to discover new experiences like never before.

Cons

- Privacy concerns

Many individuals are concerned about the privacy implications of digital technologies. Extended reality technology requires a large amount of data about the participant to function properly.

- Integration costs

High-quality extended reality experiences are costly, especially when considering headsets and haptic sensors. Not everyone has the financial means to participate.

- Physical safety

Entering a new virtual world or supplementing an old one can make it more difficult to be aware of potential threats.

Meaning of Extended Reality

First, you need to know that XR is an umbrella word for many interactive technologies that rapidly change how we interact and offer value.

We believe the following media formats/techniques are worth investigating within the scope of extended reality technologies. This is because they are frequently the practical foundations of the mediums above.

- 360° content
- 3D content
- Volumetric capture
- Photogrammetry

You may well not recognize how pervasive extended reality technology is in your daily life. It is available on many devices, and the world's top social networks make interacting with extended reality media even simpler.

For instance, the iPhone 12's LIDAR features will improve AR accuracy by making virtual items in virtual environments practically identical with the physical-world items.

The Evolution of Storytelling

In some ways, extended reality represents the next step in the development of human storytelling. Since our early beginnings, human has written stories using (1) pictograms, (2) written language (in stone), and finally (4) the ability to pen our thoughts on paper and distribute them.

Then followed the (5) radio, (6) television, (7) the internet, and the ever-present (8) consumer technology of today: phones, PCs, tablets, and other digital devices. Then we have (9) extended reality, wherein our stories, ideas, and creativity come to life on a virtual-reality space.

Interactive Digital Experience

In some way, most extended reality media formats are either interactive or experiential or both. This implies they can react to participant behavior in a variety of ways. You could be wearing a virtual reality headset an augmented reality gear (like smartglasses), or you could be immersed in a room-scale interactive experience.

In any case, the actual world now has a more fluid digital overlay thanks to AI, machine learning, and creativity. Users increasingly value experience, involvement, and a sense of belonging, as evidenced by generational patterns. And it is all driven by our data.

XR technology provides us with tremendous new opportunities to engage fans and consumers to strengthen our emotional relationships. Today, marketers use AR, VR, and MR to engage audiences in three ways:

- Using mobile phones or tablets
- Laptops or desktop computers
- Dedicated headgear such as head-mounted displays (HMDs) or room-scale projections.

Smartphones have an integrated gyroscope that lets us move our phones around to "experience" extended reality worlds or experiences. Computers enable us to enjoy more powerful virtual reality experiences that demand more processing capability, and they can be explored in different ways.

Head-mounted displays, sometimes known as "headsets," can be immersive or overlay a virtual layer on top of the real world. Hand-held controllers, gaze-based tracking, and other methods are available for interaction.

Extended reality media opens up the worlds of interactive marketing and immersive storytelling in robust ways.

Why XR is Important

- Storytelling with more depth

Extended reality gives people access to some of the most powerful storytelling approaches ever devised. The public can enjoy stories from the perspective of the person telling them through interactive marketing.

To be successful, extended reality must be backed by a strategy-driven approach, with content that is a perfect combination of marketing and deep technical understanding.

- Intuition as a source of information

Our brains have very distinct ways of thinking about the world, and extended reality provides us with novel media formats that align with our intuitive understanding of the environment around us.

We comprehend the spatial depth, emotions, and our five senses, among other things. Our stories could be narrated with more spatial information and rich sensory information thanks to extended reality, which flat media is not usually capable of.

Context is the driving force behind XR content. That is where high-fidelity storytelling thrives.

- Experience-driven

In the modern digital world, each purchase decision goes through a variety of steps, including knowledge, evaluation, and intent, all of which result in a conversion. Extended reality content may effectively engage the audience in an immersive rendition of your story or product offering, cutting through the congested media environment.

Consider being able to see the latest Adidas sneakers on your feet through augmented reality without ever having to leave your house!

Brand recall, purchase decision, and engagement have all been shown to be catalyzed by extended reality media, impacting behavior in novel and powerful ways.

XR's Role in Current Marketing

Google, Facebook, Amazon, and a slew of other tech firms are working to make extended reality available on all devices, browsers, and social networks.

Why? Because the economic contribution of extended reality technology in the years to come will be in the hundreds of billions of dollars. Popular applications such as social media, GPS, and data visualization of things like the stock market have more potential due to 5G technology and the internet of things.

The most significant barrier for businesses looking to employ extended reality is a lack of XR technical competence, XR promotional strategies, and an awareness of the economics of promising modern media campaigns.

How to Make XR Work for You

Big tech firms are spending billions of dollars on virtual reality, paving the way for widespread adoption and creative possibilities.

- Group selfie
- Increase engagement
- XR media marketing surpasses static media marketing. When you use interactive media instead of flat media, you get a 10x increase in engagement. OmniVirt's 2019 analysis found that interactive media ad formats outperform flat ads by over 3x in CTR, routinely hit around 15% engagement rate, and deliver a 13x boost in smartphone CTR after delivering over 1 billion 360/AR display advertisements.
- Bringing traditional and digital together, XR can add digital elegance to traditional stories.
- Businesses that aggressively utilize AR/VR solutions have a

newfound potential to activate storytelling via physical places and events, particularly during a socially distant epidemic.

3

NFTS IN METAVERSE

NFTs and Our Virtual Lives

It is easy to forget that the World Wide Web has only been around for about 25 years. In those 25 years, digital technology has advanced tremendously, considering its importance to our existence. It's also important to mention that this has radically altered our lives. We have progressed from a tiny network of users accessed via huge desktop computers at about 30 kbps to a large percentage of the world having easy access to the entire human knowledge carried on a smartphone in our pocket.

The flow of technological progress, on the other hand, continues. Our daily lives are becoming engulfed by the digital world. As a result, the metaverse, a concept long confined to science fiction, is beginning to shape.

Many investors and futurists characterize the metaverse in various ways, but the basic notion remains the same. The metaverse is a paradigm for living a very interconnected life. Of course, we are all interconnected right now via our smartphones, laptops, and desktop computers. The metaverse will develop when more products, services, and capabilities connect and blend. Even in today's highly connected society, this will connect us in ways that would seem unfathomable.

Most people, including Mark Zuckerberg, view the metaverse as the point at which VR can perfectly mimic social interactions. This would allow two individuals from different parts of the world to connect in a virtual space, explore the environment, and play games together. Of course, the notion of internet gaming is not new. The metaverse is the concept that internet interactions may be used to connect all aspects of our life.

NFT Technology: The Key to Metaverse

As a result, existing nonfungible token applications are only scratching the surface of the innovation. In the metaverse, everything will have to be simulated. This implies that products for sale, online items, and even online land and property must all be ownable, sellable, and transferable inside the metaverse space.

Holders of nonfungible token technology get full ownership of digital assets. You will begin to comprehend how NFTs may create a metaverse that connects society worldwide once you realize the security that possessing a digital asset on the blockchain provides. As shown by the amount paid for many digital art pieces, the notion of NFTs giving ownership over digital assets has already been embraced by the masses. The metaverse is just the virtualization of that idea.

Some NFT initiatives are already going more and more into the world of the metaverse. Most people consider blockchain gaming to be the model for an all-encompassing metaverse. Most of the principles in the metaverse have already been tested and modified in blockchain gaming.

Axie Infinity is the largest game project in the area right now and one of the largest nonfungible token projects generally. In Axies, which are comparable to Pokémon, players adopt, train, and battle. On-chain, each Axie is denoted by an NFT. As the Axies gain experience, they grow stronger and, as a result, costlier. It is possible to buy Axies and in-game products that may improve an Axies skills. In the realm of Axie Infinity, players will combat and interact with one another. Basically, Axie Infinity is a virtual environment where individuals worldwide communicate through digital objects. In some ways, it is its own constrained form of the metaverse.

Another product that dabbles in the metaverse is Xplorer's Studio, a collection of 10,000 nonfungible token astronauts. An Xplorer NFT can be used as a digital ticket to get access to a set of online tools that will assist in the creation of an online identity. Zoom backdrops, an exclusive store, a digital community wallet, and other unique features are among the functionality available. In addition, and maybe more importantly, when the NFT transactions are completed, Xplorers Studio will acquire land in a metaverse.

The purchase of virtual land in most NFTs projects is a major step forward for the metaverse paradigm. It demonstrates that value can be derived from online real estate and adds another aspect of our offline lives to blockchain technology. This dedication to broadening horizons is exactly what Xplorer Studio attempts to instill in their community and NFTs.

The metaverse is still in development. It is only now that the technology on which it will be constructed is being developed. The metaverse will begin to take shape when VR advances, the internet becomes more widely available worldwide, and blockchain gains widespread use. This new perspective is already being included in NFT projects.

Role of NFTs in Metaverse

NFTs assist the Metaverse in achieving three of the seven fundamental criteria stated by Matt Ball in his metaverse blog:

- Mass Participatory Medium: The metaverse will be a hugely interactive technology that will run simultaneously and be driven by the creative effort of millions of individuals.
- An Independent and Fair Economy - The ideal future metaverse

will be based on an autonomous economy, which is open and decentralized, allowing for worldwide job opportunities.

- Individual and Collective Agency - The metaverse will fluidly enable individual agency (i.e., you develop and produce an action) and also collective agency (i.e., people act collectively toward a common goal, such as in a mass movement), giving you a feeling of control over your metaverse experiences.

Large firms will certainly impact the metaverse by creating environments, entertainment experiences, games, and the system that supports them. On the other hand, the metaverse will be a lot more diverse and creative media than we are used to. While social media networks make it possible for anybody to create content, they are quite limiting. They decide who has access to them, what content may be generated, and who benefits from the creators' efforts.

The metaverse enables anybody to engage as an important member of the metaverse and actively shape its appearance. Users in the metaverse will be able to develop things that are greatly valued in that metaverse, define their experiences, and help define the actual appearance and feel of the metaverse.

NFTs will be a crucial component of realizing that creative participative future. In the future metaverse, NFTs can contribute to generating meaning, economic activity and offer utility.

Mass Participatory Medium

NFTs can bring millions of people into virtual environments, but it is vital to remember that the metaverse is still a tiny participatory medium. Aside from Fortnite and Roblox, most metaverses, particularly decentralized ones, have just a few thousand daily active users. In May, over 150K-250K people registered into the Dapper Labs NFT Platform of NBA Top Shot daily, whereas Axie Infinity had around 350K daily active users (DAUs).

Even though NFT ownership exceeds metaverse involvement, it is worth noting that the former can be a crucial facilitator for the latter. This is because most NFT owners (for example, Axie + TopShot Collectors) are accumulating passive digital assets that, unknown to them, may be interactively experienced and/or employed in the metaverse. We predict NFT owners to have a stronger understanding of the flexible character of the digital space as a more accessible metaverse evolves, allowing for more creative applications within virtual environments. In the metaverse space, nonfungible tokens are currently being used to showcase digital art galleries as membership tokens for exclusive access to events, virtual fashion, digital sporting events, and interactive infrastructures.

Luckily, the nonfungible token space's technology and innovation assist in onboarding and evangelizing NFT ownership regardless of one's cryptocurrency knowledge or expertise. The tools for creating, discovering, acquiring, showcasing, and selling NFTs are crucial onramps into the larger NFT space. Still, they may also be used to enroll digital citizens into the metaverse.

NFTs will ultimately become ubiquitous in gaming and metaverses. You will reach a point when you do not even notice using a nonfungible token in the virtual environment. To arrive here, we will need early testing from metaverses like ours and continuous technical improvement, but we are well on our way.

These instruments can be divided into four groups:

- Minting Platforms

Systems that facilitate the creation of digital assets in the form of nonfungible tokens are known as minting platforms. Bitski and Art Blocks are two minting platforms that enable companies and creatives to mint and sell main Nonfungible tokens.

- Marketplace

Marketplaces are areas where NFTs may be found, posted for sale, and bought. Rarible and OpenSea are open platforms that accept any approved protocol NFT, whereas MakersPlace and SuperRare are curated marketplaces.

- NFT Social Networks

These are decentralized online social networks for displaying and discovering nonfungible tokens. NFT Bank enables users to track and get alerts on collectors' nonfungible token wallets and changes creative monetization.

- Wallets

Wallets are a person's central hub and storage location for their nonfungible tokens. Wallets may one day become the virtual identity that may be transported from one Metaverse to the next. Collectors can display and send NFTs and also cryptocurrency using wallets like Rainbow and Phantom.

Independent and Fair Economy

The future metaverse will include a vibrant economy that will revolutionize resource allocation while allowing members to locate a "job" via virtual labor. Virtual economies arise in games like World of Warcraft and Fortnite, but they are often centralized, closed, proprietary, and extractive. People could be restricted (or worse, removed) from economies, standards can be modified unilaterally, and players' financial circumstances (such as currency supply) remain hidden. Users in Fortnite, for instance, have no realistic method of determining a skin's actual scarcity.

As a result of leveraging NFTs, the Open metaverse(s) will feature virtual economies that can increase size and complexity while also infiltrating the virtual and real worlds. NFTs provide players in virtual economies property rights that are enforced by irreversible code. The value of a digital asset or the tokenomics of its coin will be visible and understood to users, allowing for economic predictability that will encourage creativity, development, and resource allocation in support of a healthy virtual economy.

We anticipate open metaverses to profit from quicker development, higher innovation, and more effective use of limited resources, as in the physical environment economies that tilt their arc toward openness.

Nonfungible tokens that give actual user utility and function as an incentive for metaverse users who give back to the Metaverse they occupy will be created to help mainstream in this virtual economic space. The play-to-earn gaming category, NFT DeFi, and DAOs are examples of this coming to reality.

- **Play to Earn**

NFT-based games allow metaverse users to earn virtual environment currencies and items exchanged for other digital assets or fiat currency. ZED RUN, a virtual gaming startup that enables participants to purchase, trade, breed, and race NFT horses in the play-to-earn sector, is at the front line. Participants may profit from their horses (which can cost anywhere from $130 to $45,000) as their worth rises by breeding them and winning races. With a quickly growing group of 50,000 participants in ZED RUN, we believe the next Bob Baffert will be discovered training and racing NFT horses on digital racetrack across the metaverse that will be televised on Twitch, rather than at Churchill Downs preparing 1,000-pound horses for NBC.

Animated horse racing has existed for years, but what ZED RUN has accomplished via digital ownership has profoundly altered the dynamic. ZED RUN includes a captivating play-to-earn element and NFTs that show great value in response to user actions. A racehorse that routinely wins races, for instance, will certainly gain in value and develop a greater emotional bond with its owner. ZED RUN NFTs not only symbolizes value and yield, but they also stimulate emotion in a way that has never been done before with something virtual.

- **NFT DeFi**

The overlap with Decentralized Finance (DeFi) allows nonfungible tokens to be borrowed, exchanged, and fractionalized, allowing digital items to be important not just within their particular virtual worlds but also outside of them, such as with physical assets and fiat currencies. This novel convergence of finance, digital environment assets, and basic financial systems provides metaverse members new financial prospects. Through Decentralized Finance, art, for instance, is reshaping NFT asset ownership. NFT holders can use Fractional to create tokenized fractional ownership of NFTs. The fractionalized token's holders also have control over the NFT it owns. Fractionalized NFTs provide liquidity to NFT owners while increasing the number of people who can participate in NFTs and virtual economies. This is significant since it will result in a more liquid and strong NFT market. Consequently, combining nonfungible tokens with new financial instruments will allow better price discovery, greater liquidity, and greater participation.

- **Decentralized Autonomous Organizations (DAO)**

A DAO is an organization with no central governance and laws defined and executed by a computer algorithm. Decisions within a DAO are made from the bottom up and voted on by token owners in the community. The community owns, governs, and manages DAOs jointly. Yield Guild Games (YGG) depicts the various ways in which capital will be formed due to a metaverse that allows free economic activity with nonfungible tokens. YGG is a Decentralized Autonomous Organization (DAO), establishing itself as a crucial player in the metaverse space, using its funds and wealth of scholars to ignite virtual economies. YGG buys nonfungible token resources (including land, horses, and Axis) from virtual environments and then loans them to scholars who use them in their virtual environments to earn money. YGG keeps a modest percentage of the Scholars' earnings. YGG's objective is to build the largest digital world economy by fostering a lively society, maximizing the utility of its public-owned NFT assets, and distributing profits with token holders. In the digital landscape, YGG will use NFTs to serve two main functions:

- Create a global network of metaverse users who will devote their time and energy to virtual environments in exchange for in-world benefits.
- Produce revenue by renting or selling YGG-owned assets for a profit.

The value of these transactions will be distributed to YGG's DAO token holders. Additionally, 45 percent of this DAO's tokens are kept for community members to incentivize and reward people who make substantial contributions to the community. As a result, YGG has created an organization that encourages metaverse involvement and awards metaverses that give their communities the best chance to profit from a fair and open virtual economy. YGG is serving as a collective force for metaverse developers to create virtual economy systems that accept nonfungible tokens, openness, and transparency to profit from YGG's robust community of virtual environment settlers.

Individual and Collective Agency

One of the essential characteristics of the metaverse is that it gives people a sense of agency. Users must be encouraged to believe they have control over and influence over their metaverse activities. Nonfungible tokens play a crucial role in providing metaverses with identity, community, and diversity. Users can use nonfungible tokens to create areas in the metaverse, own them, and transfer ownership of the areas they have worked extremely hard to develop.

- Identity

Nonfungible tokens allow players to create compatible avatars that mirror their real or imagined selves. They can stay present and consistent as they travel through the different metaverses.

- Variety

Nonfungible tokens allow for endless innovation and a vast range of digital assets to be used in the metaverse space, empowering people to build and shape their own metaverse experiences.

Projects like Meebits, the Bored Ape Yacht Club, and CryptoPunks show how nonfungible tokens can have collective agency in the metaverse space. Ownership of one of these nonfungible tokens avatar entails the transfer of an avatar to the metaverse and membership in a digital society where discourse and activities take place across the real world, social media networks, and virtual environments. The Bored Ape Yacht Club community has made baseball caps and gathered together for a fun time in the real world. In contrast, they have manufactured digital hoodie clothes in the metaverse and run a perfectly functioning riverboat casino. The joint community of these avatars shapes the events and landscapes of the metaverses they choose to interact with.

While nonfungible tokens hold a lot of promise for the metaverse, they have been hampered by current infrastructural constraints:

- Infrastructure for scalability
- Tools for developers
- Lack of Metadata standards

Consequently, nonfungible token collectors face significant transaction costs, and developers find it challenging to create NFT-based apps. As a result, some of the best nonfungible token applications in the Metaverse are yet to be developed.

4

METAVERSE INVESTMENT

Metaverse Business Application

W e believe the metaverse will open up a wide range of income opportunities across many industries, especially for firms that develop virtual products and associated components, ultra-realistic visuals, chips and processors, and related software.

Developer/Creator Markets

A healthy metaverse needs a large intermediary developer base that provides experiences and accessories, just as Apple established an environment where developers sell their applications. If the $200 billion collected by Apple's App Store developers between 2008 and 2020 is any indicator, the metaverse's market may be huge. Roblox developers made $328.7 million in 2020 and $248.7 million in the first half of 2021 alone. On the creator side, there are comparable opportunities: Over the previous three years, Alphabet's YouTube has given out a sum of $30 billion to artists. Developer earnings are frequently split with the social media or video game platforms themselves, which is problematic. Metaverse platforms are expected to reap comparable economics as Apple, which earns 30% of app store profits.

Ads

Social media networks are well-known for providing free services to their users, with focused ads driving the majority of their earning. Gaming businesses continually pursue a similar approach, providing consumers with free-to-play experiences supported by advertisements and in-game purchases. In-platform advertisements for real-world physical products as well as advertising for virtual metaverse-based items, such as games, accessories, experiences, and other items, are expected to follow a similar approach in metaverse experiences. The metaverse, based on statistics, may be a $500 billion market disruptor for the worldwide media advertising business.

Social Commerce

E-commerce systems may expand beyond selling things on websites to providing their items in simulated malls, where people may buy digital stuff for their virtual existence and real-life objects that can be dispatched to their front door. In a simulated mall, customers may browse goods with peers, speak with an influencer about the item, and virtually try out the product before actually buying it. In many respects, it is the next evolution of e-commerce, or the interaction of e-commerce and social media, that, based on statistics, will produce $475 billion annually.

Digital Events

Beyond being a video game, Fortnite became an online hub for players who wished to digitally attend events, view movie trailer premieres and watch films during the COVID-19 crisis. In the future, digital events are expected to be a key product inside the metaverse. You may, for instance, virtually attend events, cinema, games, or e-sports events with your pals while still being able to enjoy the comforts of your own home. Returning to Ariana Grande's virtual performance at a Fortnite concert, the artist was paid an astounding $20 million for her performance. The worldwide virtual events industry is expected to be worth $94 billion, with profits shared between content developers (such as movie studios, professional sports teams, and musicians) and metaverse platforms that host the events.

Hardware

VR and AR headsets, graphic chips, and omnidirectional treadmills are just a few examples of big-tech hardware that will undoubtedly play a key part in the creation of an interactive virtual metaverse. The hardware industry might rise from $31 billion in 2021 to $297 billion by 2024. The possibility for virtual reality technology in the metaverse alone may be worth more than $100 billion.

Wallets and Applications

New services will arise when cash transactions shift to the metaverse. People will have to quickly switch between fiat and digital currencies, buy products with digital currencies, and keep track of their digital transactions. These businesses will most likely request transaction fees, foreign/virtual exchange conversions, and custodial services in exchange. FinTechs, particularly those focusing on blockchain, might be crucial in enabling these transactions and assuring legitimate ownership.

Virtual Products Sale

A virtual product is a product that exists solely in digital form. It might be a virtual depiction of an actual product or a product that only resides in the digital landscape. While these items may not be "real" in the sense that we normally think of reality, they are certainly "real" enough for real people to invest real cash in them.

Virtual products may have clear uses for many businesses. It is not difficult to envision someone purchasing an expensive virtual Ferrari to gain an advantage in a virtual racing simulator. Using a high-end suit in a virtual setting has the same effect as using one in reality.

Certain advantages of a Chalupa Supreme (a traditional flatbread), do not seem to transition well into a virtual world. It is more difficult to envision how a firm like Taco Bell would use virtual items. That did not prevent them from producing and selling virtual items worth thousands of dollars in the previous month.

The message is clear. If you can produce and sell things in the actual world, you can certainly make and sell them in the virtual world as well. And the worth of such things will only rise as we move closer to an interactive multiverse.

Reaching Tremendous Audiences

Consider it for a moment. How desperately do you want your items and brand to be included in a blockbuster movie or at a sporting event? The video game business is bigger than the sports and cinema industries combined on a global scale. With a digital skin in Fortnite or a product promotion in Animal Crossing, you would reach a larger audience.

Even if you cannot earn a lot selling virtual items, you can start leveraging significant brand equity gains right now. Whether or not your product has an application that corresponds to one of the modern virtual environments, you have a brand that may be used on virtual clothing, signage, paintings, and other products.

These audiences are not just huge, but they are also likely to differ in major ways from your conventional brand audience. Nonfungible tokens and virtual products are being used by businesses to reach out to younger audiences. Two-thirds of Fortnite gamers are between the ages of 24 and 24. Roblox's user population is considerably younger, with two-thirds of its users being under sixteen.

Luxury businesses, for example, see value in enabling virtual users to buy virtual editions of their high-priced items before they can do so in the physical environment.

Marketing in the Metaverse

Digital marketers must keep up with the most recent technology advancements. Knowing the metaverse and its potential is part of this.

Marketers have to realize that the metaverse is not simply a fad; it appears to be here to stay and on its way to becoming the next big thing.

What strategies may marketers use to adapt as the metaverse grows? First and foremost, marketers must remember the importance of millennials and Generation Z as a target market. Certain kinds of metaverses, like games such as Roblox and technologies like virtual reality, are also popular among these generations. Let us look at how advertising can be conducted in the metaverse.

- Parallel metaverse marketing within real-life marketing

Develop promotional experiences that connect with real-life events or are similar to what your company presently does in the physical world. For instance, AB InBev's beer firm Stella Artois worked with Zed Run to develop a Tamagotchi-inspired experience coupled with the Kentucky Derby. They did so since Stella Artois, a brand of AB InBev is known for supporting sporting events, particularly horse racing. As a result, developing a virtual platform where NFT horses may be sold, raced, and bred appears to be a natural next step for them.

- Immersive experience

You can provide digital marketing in the metaverse space. Bidstack, a game ad tech firm, shifted from physical-world outdoor marketing to virtual billboard marketing.

However, virtual billboards are not the only option. Because metaverses are engaging and interactive by nature, it is ideal to capitalize on this by providing a similar interactive experience with your promotions and marketing efforts. Instead of merely posting commercials, offer branded installations and events that people may engage with.

We have seen early adopters provide an interactive experience to their consumers, like a Lil Nas X performance in Roblox, Gucci Garden experience visits, and Warner Bros.' advertising of 'In the Heights' with a digital version of the Washington Heights neighborhood. Partnerships with the Roblox metaverse and other metaverses have now shown new revenue sources for businesses.

*@ Nat : fortunes
@ Lee : jukebox tokens.

- Make collectibles available

Individuals like collectibles, and the metaverse provides them with yet another platform to do so. You may reproduce the experience in the metaverse by providing products or unique items that can only be obtained in the metaverse.

The Collector's Room, for instance, is available in the Gucci Garden Roblox experience. In the metaverse, it enables users to gather limited-edition Gucci products. Gucci made a total of 286,000,000 Robux from the game's early sales of collectible products.

- Engage with existing communities

The public generally dislikes advertising. As businesses aim to break into the metaverse, they mustn't irritate those who are already there. You will also need the favorable feedback of these users because you will be marketing to them.

Note that you may not simply enter a new system without taking into consideration the new layout. For instance, in Roblox, businesses gain more traction when they collaborate with members of the Roblox developer community to create products and experiences. Likewise, when O2 put up a performance on Fortnite, they teamed up with developers who were experts on the game.

Consider this a form of influencer marketing. Community members become key aspects of the implementation of the marketing since user-generated content is vital.

@Andrew

- Continuously experiment

Marketers are in an incredible time. While some core principles can help marketers determine what techniques and methods to use, the metaverse is still a relatively young platform with plenty of potential for experimentation. Best practices are still being defined, and paradigms are still being developed in their entirety. This provides marketers a lot of flexibility to explore new things and be creative in their strategies.

Metaverse ETF

Metaverse ETF is a basket of assets that trade on a stock market. This ETF allows investors to participate in some organizations that are currently making the metaverse a reality or poised to do so in the nearest future.

Matthew Ball, a futurist and trader, and other entrepreneurs, including Jacob Navok, CEO of Genvid Technologies, founded the Metaverse ETF. They claim to have done the legwork of studying the metaverse, so you do not have to, and they are promoting the idea that the metaverse can democratize everything in the process. In this scenario, they are decentralizing metaverse investments by inventing an ETF that anyone can invest in and profit from the metaverse's rewards.

Bloomberg recently projected the market size of the metaverse to reach $800 billion. With this ETF, investors would understand the worth of the metaverse daily, even while it is still in its early stages. While the metaverse is science fiction, it is conceivable to anticipate which firms will play a crucial part in bringing it to fruition.

An ETF assembles a bundle based on an index that includes a wide range, or as many as you like, of various public business equities. An investor can outsource their choice to this index if they want access to a subject or area but do not have the competence to choose all of the individual stocks."

How to Invest in Metaverse

If you are a seasoned investor, you already know that it is never too late to get in on the ground floor. While most of what the metaverse is might still be a mystery, there are currently ways for individuals to invest in the metaverse's prospects passively.

According to Bloomberg Intelligence, the metaverse industry would be worth USD 800 billion by 2024, indicating that this may be a profitable field to invest in. We will look at four different ways you can incorporate the metaverse into your investment plan.

Stocks in the Metaverse

Purchasing "metaverse stocks" is one method that people interested in the metaverse might invest in it. Holdings in publicly listed firms participating in the creation of the metaverse are known as metaverse stocks.

Considering that it is at the vanguard of developing the metaverse, Facebook is an excellent example of a firm whose stock you may buy if you want to invest in it. Facebook's CEO, Mark Zuckerberg, has stated that he does not want the firm to be identified as a social media firm. He likes it to be recognized as a metaverse firm instead.

Suppose you do not wish to invest in Facebook. The social media firm already has an Oculus virtual reality headset and only recently introduced its first smart glasses in collaboration with Ray-Ban augmented reality to expand its AR platform. In that case, other businesses like Microsoft, Unity Software, Roblox, Amazon, Walt Disney, and Nvidia aim to play a part in the metaverse's evolution.

Metaverse Exchange-traded Funds (ETFs)

Alternatively, investors may purchase a metaverse ETF to acquire exposure to the rapidly developing metaverse business. An exchange-traded fund (ETF) is a collection of assets that trade on a stock market.

Individuals can buy into a metaverse stock ETF to invest in firms already creating the metaverse or firms in a strong position to do so in the future. For instance, the Roundhill Ball Metaverse ETF (META) was developed to enable anybody to invest in and profit from the metaverse. Investors may gain exposure to businesses including Nvidia, Microsoft, Roblox, Tencent, Unity, and Amazon with Roundhill Investment's ETF.

Virtual World Tokens

Virtual world tokens (VWTs) are virtual tokens that are associated with the VR landscape. Virtual world tokens may be used to purchase land and in-game treasures such as avatars in the virtual environment.

The Metaverse Index (MVI) token, for instance, is a virtual world token that gives owners access to a variety of tokens from cryptocurrency projects in fields including NFTs, virtual environments, and online gaming. The metaverse Index token may be thought of as a metaverse ETF for the cryptocurrency market.

Decentraland's coins are yet another example. Decentraland is a VR platform that enables users to purchase land, communicate with one another, and play games. It is the nonfungible token ecosystem's largest virtual environment, and its virtual land is reflected on the Ethereum network by the NFT LAND.

MANA and LAND are the two tokens used in Decentraland. LAND is an NFT that symbolizes all plots of land on the network, whereas MANA is the network's native governance token utilized for transactions.

NFTs in the Metaverse

The growth and acceptance of the metaverse will be aided by blockchain-supported metaverses that will most likely use nonfungible tokens and cryptocurrency assets. This is because a working metaverse will enable people to navigate their avatars and virtual assets from one reality to another in a fluid and fast way.

Nonfungible tokens are digital assets that reflect a variety of unique products like art, in-game content, and collectibles. Individuals may now buy virtual pieces of land and even create their settings using nonfungible tokens thanks to sites like Decentraland and The Sandbox. We should expect additional investment possibilities in this sector as we get closer to the metaverse being a reality.

Metaverse Players

Metaverse stocks have a lot of promise from an investor's perspective. This section highlighted six metaverse stocks and one exchange-traded fund (ETF) that are potential major winners in the next wave of technology.

Fastly

Latency, or data lag, has arisen as a result of cloud computing and decentralization. People encounter this when they click a link in their search engine and wait for the next page or procedure to load. The problem is the data's travel distance, which is not a huge matter if they look up the weather. The data lag can appear to be a pain in the neck if they are in a self-driving car or performing robotic surgery.

Fastly (FSLY, $40.44) is a business that specializes in edge computing and technology. FSLY runs an edge computing infrastructure-as-a-service (IaaS) system that moves servers and other devices closer to the point where data is generated. The technology used by Fastly can transport 145 gigabytes of data per second across 28 nations. Essentially, it aids in the reduction of decentralization's lag time and latency.

The firm's services appear to be popular among businesses. Fastly has had rapid income growth since its inception over a couple of years, with earnings increasing 14% year over year in the last quarter.

The metaverse will require many edge computing systems, similar to cloud computing. Consider the massive data transfer required to build a virtual environment that people can interact with in real-time. These types of transactions would be impossible to carry out without edge computing and firms like Fastly.

FSLY is an attractive growth play on the ongoing rise of cloud computing, in addition to its potential as a metaverse stock. Fastly is now affordable than it has been in a long time, thanks to a m... wreck-induced decrease in shares.

Nvidia

Nvidia (NVDA, $207.16) has long been regarded as one of the finest long-term semiconductor investments. Its entrance into the realms of artificial intelligence (AI) and other fast-processing devices makes it a prominent participant in the metaverse stock market, which is unsurprising.

The chipsets developed by NVDA are already being used in a variety of servers and other centralized computers that do heavy computations. Edge computing solutions offered by companies like Fastly fall into this category. Given its leading position and the need to respond quickly, Nvidia is likely to be a major winner from the metaverse development.

Another factor for its bright future is the imminent acquisition of ARM Holdings from SoftBank Group. ARM is a prominent player in the patents and software that enable the integration of chips into computer systems. NVDA will be able to expand its end-to-end environment as a result of the acquisition. To put it another way, it can immediately integrate its graphics processing unit (GPU) and sophisticated processors into additional systems, boosting computing capacity. And the metaverse will require this level of processing power to function.

While its approximately $40 billion acquisition of ARM is far from certain — U.K. authorities are among the most recent to express antitrust concerns – NVDA remains a possible metaverse winner. After all, its processors are still the gold standard for high-speed computations and processing.

Roblox

A video game may appear like an unusual choice for Gucci to start an exclusive event. Still, it demonstrates the metaverse's looming potential and how Roblox (RBLX, $75.55) is laying the foundation for it.

RBLX appears to be a video game on the outside. A highly popular one. In the second quarter, the firm had 43.2 million daily active users who accumulated 9.7 billion hours of interaction.

The problem is that it is not truly a single game. Roblox relies on third-party developers to create games, content, and other forms of entertainment for its participants. The company earns income by trading virtual currency, which gamers can purchase games, activities, content, and even virtual clothes for their avatars, such as Gucci bags.

Roblox has already built the foundation for the metaverse inside its game. And it is just getting bigger. Roblox CEO Dave Baszucki said on a newly released earnings call with investors that the company's system welcomes kids and, at the same time, welcomes adults. Roblox envisions its platform as a virtual space where interactive activities, such as concerts, are happening, just as play is going on right now.

RBLX is spending a lot of money on skills and deals to build its version of the metaverse. One notable example is its acquisition of Guilded, a platform that connects multiple gaming groups. Roblox's platform and investment plan continue to generate rising income for the firm. The company's sales increased by 126 percent year over year in the last quarter. This follows a year-over-year earnings rise of 140 percent in the first quarter.

This metaverse stock might be a strong addition to portfolios due to its large metaverse investment share in the foundations of the next generation of technology.

Facebook

When Facebook (FB, $339.39 - Oct 2021) bought virtual reality firm Oculus in 2014, it set the foundation for its metaverse ambition. Overall, Facebook has struggled with the division of its social media activities, and it has always appeared to be a trend business for the company. Zuckerberg, on the other hand, may be having the last laugh.

Facebook released a public edition of Horizon Workrooms, a new Oculus software. Users may join in meetings through avatars using the company's virtual reality headsets. They can see and interact with their computer screens, keyboards, and virtual whiteboards.

Facebook appears to be one of the first to market with such services. In a newly-released blog post, Zuckerberg stated, "Collaborating will be one of the major ways people utilize the metaverse in the future." Considering the recent increase in remote work agreements resulting from COVID-19, this might be a big victory for Facebook in the nearest future.

Longer-term prospects may also be promising because Facebook is currently a collection of communities through its different applications and communication channels. It's ideal for the business to shift to the metaverse.

This may provide a secondary source of promotion revenue or charges for content providers within its network and system in the future. That is a long way off, although considering Facebook's technology leadership and present first-mover status in work-related applications, the metaverse stock might arrive sooner than others.

Even better, Facebook is a safe bet on the metaverse's expansion. The company's profitability and cash flow generation are undeniable. Conservative investors may feel more at ease as they consider the topic.

Autodesk

Autodesk (ADSK, $285.17) is well known for its groundbreaking AutoCAD program, first released in the 1980s. Engineers, architects, designers, and scholars may use this program to digitally design and develop buildings, objects, and construction projects in 2D and 3D. It is the industry's standard technology, and most infrastructure projects use it at some point throughout their lifespan.

That software is still the company's most successful product. Developers have begun to use ADSK's software to create and design virtual environments for gaming and entertainment, which is where things become intriguing for ADSK. The company currently has a suite of tools to render 3D animation, develop and launch virtual structures, and create VR and AR environments. In the most recent quarter, earnings from this area (M&E) increased by 10% year over year.

Autodesk is a logical match and quickly establishes itself as the go-to platform for developers interested in the metaverse and its creation. The greatest news is that Autodesk has focused on the profitable software-as-a-service (SaaS) model, with consistent revenue contributing 98 percent of total sales in the latest quarter. Those recurrent sales have also resulted in a substantial profit margin. In the second quarter, earnings increased by 23.5 percent. ADSK generated $186 million in free cash flow (the cash left after a firm has cleared all its expenses, interest on debt, taxes, and future investments to grow its business).

Autodesk is a great pick for investors searching for metaverse stocks because of its extensive experience in 3D design.

Shopify

One of the most important aspects of the metaverse is that its developers desire a thriving economy inside its virtual borders. Assets, cash, and the capacity for content developers to be compensated must all be digitalized. That is where Shopify (SHOP, $1,355.78), an e-commerce expert, comes in.

SHOP is well-known as the company that enables businesses to create websites and does business online. Since its early introduction, Shopify has grown its toolkit and services to include a variety of ancillary products that small companies require to succeed.

It is happening now with the digital and metaverse economies. Shopify has taken two significant actions that relate to the possibilities of metaverse commerce. One example is the purchase of the augmented reality app Primer. Users may experience the consequences of purchase or project in their environment directly. It offers SHOP a strong tool in the metaverse, allowing members to build up future businesses or shopping experiences in the digital world.

Introducing a new nonfungible token platform will enable digital artists to sell art and other content to people directly. The Chicago Bulls were the first to put the product to the test, releasing limited edition nonfungible tokens of the team's 1991 championship rings. The two projects perfectly position Shopify to link into the metaverse and offer it a foundation in the virtual environment's prospective commercial goals.

SHOP is still doing what it does best – solving e-commerce problems for businesses – as these future ambitions unfold. And, as the top producer of such technology, shares of this metaverse stock are quite secure.

Roundhill Ball Metaverse ETF

Considering the metaverse's trendy nature, it is not unexpected that an ETF has already been established to monitor the project. It is the Roundhill Ball Metaverse ETF (META, $14.16) in this scenario. And, to be honest, it could be the finest method for investors to profit from the virtual space's idea and development.

META was created by Matthew Ball, a futurist and venture entrepreneur, and others to symbolize the whole metaverse spectrum. META manages everything from architecture and user interface to content creation and user experience. In reality, there are fifty distinct stocks. Cloud solutions, gaming systems, and computer component stocks account for almost 70 percent of the ETF's overall portfolio. Nvidia, Microsoft (MSFT), and China's gaming behemoth Tencent (TCEHY) are among the top individual holdings.

When it comes to META, there are a few things to keep in mind. For starters, it is brand new. The exchange-traded fund (ETF) was just recently introduced. Before investing in a new fund, it is usually good to wait to amass assets and trading volume. When it comes to theme and specialist funds, this is particularly true. Regardless, the ETF has already amassed over $100 million in assets. META's 30-day average daily volume is about 250,000 shares, indicating that activity has begun to rise.

Second, investors must be aware of the price. META now charges 0.75 percent in yearly costs. Even for a specialized fund, it is a little on the expensive side. In contrast, the iShares Virtual Work and Life Multisector ETF (IWFH), modeled around the metaverse, charges only 0.47 percent in costs.

With those two drawbacks in mind, META might be a solid option for investors wanting to profit from metaverse stocks from a wide perspective.

Best Metaverse Investment Stocks in Categories

Considering the technological challenges and financial benefits, it is doubtful that a single business would develop the metaverse. The metaverse must be so interactive that it is desirable to interact in a certain location or for a specified purpose. This will necessitate the use of technology from many sources.

High-performance computing, data services, next-generation networking, virtual networks, cryptocurrencies, and identity services, among numerous other technologies, will be required for a real version of the metaverse.

Let's now take a look at the major technology categories for investment in the metaverse.

Large Tech, Computing, Gaming, and Digital Assets are the four categories in classifying the investable assets associated with these sectors.

Big Tech Investment

Facebook(FB)

Microsoft (MSFT)

Alphabet (GOOG)

Amazon (AMZN)

Apple (AAPL)

The FAAMG stocks, commonly known as Big Tech, are expected to handle the heavy lifting. They have the skills and resources needed to design the metaverse's architecture. Their key income sources (platforms, search, software, and cloud computing) will fund their metaverse activities and function as critical metaverse elements.

They also have the advantage of long time horizons, allowing them to 'fail' in ways that would obliterate smaller businesses. They are doomed to fail until they succeed. The 'disruptor' class of enterprises will invent the metaverse's features, while Big Tech will provide the framework.

Facebook (FB)

In June 2021, Mark Zuckerberg disclosed the next phase of Facebook, stating that "in the next couple of years," Facebook would shift from a social media firm to a metaverse firm. On the other hand, Facebook has been laying the groundwork for the metaverse for quite some time.

The metaverse will have an economy, thanks to Facebook's creation of a digital token for payments. What firm fully comprehends avatars than Facebook? On Instagram, many users have already made avatars of themselves.

Facebook is in charge of bringing the real and digital worlds together. Facebook Inc. may be getting a new coat of paint. The firm is looking to change its name in the coming weeks, according to a report on technology news site the Verge, to indicate its recent focus on developing the metaverse. According to nation world, the firm plans to hire 10,000 workers from the European Union over the next five years to build the metaverse.

Microsoft (MSFT)

Metaverse applications are possible because of Microsoft's Azure cloud computing system. The firm's metaverse technological stack is built on cloud and edge computing. Sam George, a Microsoft executive, recently wrote that they are best positioned to put this complete stack together. Their audacious objective is to make this stack more linked and smooth over time so you can simply travel up and down the layers that allow metaverse apps.

George refers to Azure Digital Twin, a layer in Microsoft's metaverse stack that can simulate an item, technology, or full area and keep the digital twins current and up-to-date using Azure IoT.

Assume that a Ford executive is attempting to identify possible obstacles at a factory in Detroit. Rather than boarding a plane and going to Detroit, he enters the metaverse and finds himself on the factory's bottom floor. Real-time digital twins of machinery are in front of him, with analyses of their energy cost per hour, maintenance expenses, and productivity displayed above them. The CEO could make certain choices since he knows the digital representations are correct courtesy of Azure Digital Twin.

The integrity of the metaverse requires synchronization between the virtual and actual worlds. For clarity, Azure Digital Twins is simply one component of the firm's metaverse technological stack. Microsoft is one of the few firms that is fully equipped for the metaverse.

Google (GOOG)

Google is an intriguing metaverse investment because of its exposure to the world's data and AI potential. Designing for the metaverse is an excellent example of why Google restructured in 2015. Creating the parent company, 'Alphabet,' enabled the firm to develop new technologies without detracting from its core businesses of search and marketing.

Google initiated a not-so-secret effort dubbed Google X, now known as X Development, in 2010 to improve life and commodities by a factor of ten. The Moonshot Factory is effectively a company within Alphabet's walls. X has spawned hundreds of various moonshot initiatives since its inception.

Google Glass, a VR-enabled set of goggles that eventually 'failed,' was one of these moonshots. Nevertheless, it was more of a public relations blunder than a failure. Google's interest in virtual reality and augmented reality is only the tip of the iceberg.

The firm is undoubtedly the most advanced in terms of autonomous driving technology. DeepMind, a Google affiliate, recently developed an AI technology to predict a protein's 3D structure based on its amino acid sequence. Google opted to make the information available to the scientific world to speed up research.

But do not forget about Google's main sources of income: Search, YouTube, and Cloud. Data, entertainment, and connection will define the next phase of the internet. For years, "Google" and "internet" have been interchangeable terms.

Given Google's vision, AI skills, and on-the-ground presence, it is difficult to conceive a scenario where the metaverse exists without Google contributing substantially.

Amazon (AMZN)

Without computational elements and cloud technologies, a fully realized metaverse is impossible. This is where Amazon enters the picture. Over a third of the public cloud industry is controlled by Amazon Web Services. It offers cloud computing services to the majority of businesses.

Firms who wish to have virtual real estate in the metaverse would have to compensate Amazon for it, much like they did in Web 2.0. The gaming sector is a good illustration of this reliance. AWS is used by more than 90% of the world's largest public game firms.

For Amazon, the intersection of the metaverse, gaming, and AWS will be a money-printing bonanza. Nevertheless, there will be more possibilities in a decentralized world, and we assume Ether or an Ether-like blockchain to offer some type of structure in collaboration with Amazon.

Amazon and Google, we assume, will also contribute substantially to the metaverse. It may not have a clear metaverse plan like Facebook and Microsoft, but it will play an important role.

Amazon's current offerings already include physical and virtual elements. As the rate of blending increases, Amazon will reap the benefits.

Apple (AAPL)

To complete the finest FAAMG investment stocks, we have included Apple, but it is uncertain what function the firm will play in the metaverse. In a decentralized Web3 ecosystem, the App Store's dominance on applications is threatened.

John Riccitiello, CEO of Unity Software, recently stated that the metaverse simply could not operate as a gated community in a world populated with artists, designers, and innovators. The idea that anyone firm can pursue that goal is filled with arrogance.

Apple is also lagging behind Facebook and Microsoft in the augmented reality and virtual reality device industry. This put them farther behind in developing a metaverse digital platform.

But you would be foolish to gamble against Apple; it has consistently delivered when we have questioned, "What is next?" The Apple world extends well beyond iPhone and Mac suites, with the iPad, AirPods, and the AppleWatch.

Hardware components will be required in the metaverse's initial phases, and we will not be left behind if Apple scores another home run in this sector.

Investment Stocks to Buy in Computing

Nvidia (NVDA)

Advanced Micro Devices (AMD)

Qualcomm (QCOM)

TSMC is a Tai(TSM)

Since Big Tech is the foundation of the metaverse, the computer and semiconductor investments in this section are the foundation of the metaverse's architecture. The most refined iteration of the metaverse, as earlier said, is an entirely interactive one. Next-generation graphics will be required.

Nvidia (NVDA) and Advanced Micro Devices (AMD) offer CPUs and GPUs that allow high-level computing and expert visualization. Nvidia is, without a doubt, the greatest 'pure-play' metaverse investment available. The AI and supercomputing required to make this a reality are powered by its main business products.

If you like to get even more involved, think about buying TSMC (TSM). This firm manufactures the chips sold by Nvidia and AMD. The last company on this list, Qualcomm (QCOM), is unique in this group.

Qualcomm develops wireless-related chips, software, and services. Its processors deliver high-performance processing for mobile apps and devices like smartphones, robots, virtual reality, and augmented reality.

Best Gaming Investment Stock

Unity Software (U)

Roblox (RBLX)

Sea (SE)

Zynga (ZNGA)

The game industry has a greater understanding of the metaverse than anybody else. These firms are the gateway into the metaverse world; they have been developing virtual environments for years and have made numerous variations on what works and what doesn't.

This tendency has been driven by the rise of in-game engine companies such as Roblox (RBLX), Unity Software (U), and Epic Games, which empower players. Participants may utilize these systems to play video games and develop them using no-code applications.

The user has progressed from enjoying the game to producing it and will ultimately be a part of it. Innovation is decreasing the bandwidth. We will scoff at the thought of using a controller to enjoy a game in the future.

Our understanding of the term "video game" will most likely evolve as well. We will stop thinking of them as "games" and start thinking of them as "experiences" as bandwidth reduces and gets more interactive.

Digital Assets Investment Stocks

Square (SQ)

PayPal (PYPL)

Bitcoin

Ethereum

The metaverse and cryptocurrency were built for one other. We understand that money is a technology that will alter dramatically as Web3 transitions. There is potential there. The Ethereum Blockchain technology has the potential to enable initiatives like DeFi apps that eliminate the need for banks and other financial intermediaries. Nonfungible tokens might be used to establish digital asset ownership.

Bitcoin's infrastructure and monetary policy might flourish in a more digital world, reducing the Federal Reserve's role. Layer 2 technology, like the Lightning Network, will allow for quick and safe fund transfers between two entities without requiring third-party control.

The price of Bitcoin and Ethereum would benefit from these uses. Other people will desire to utilize those valuable products as more developers build on their networks and generate great offerings. They will require the blockchain governance token to pay for those offers. Thus they will purchase bitcoin as an asset.

Because bitcoin's demand exceeds supply, continuous or growing demand for the asset should drive its price to rise. Square (SQ) was also added to this category since it is a publicly listed Fintech business that fully embraces the possibilities of cryptocurrency.

In the future years, PayPal (PYPL) will do everything Square does. It has the potential audience and resources to steal Square's technology without paying a cost, i.e., it may be second to new products and services.

The Cash App and PayPal's Venmo will almost certainly support it in the metaverse, irrespective of traded money.

Other Investment Stocks to Consider in the Metaverse

Disney (DIS)

Snapchat (SNAP)

Zoom (ZM)

Twitter (TWTR)

CrowdStrike (CRWD)

Okta (OKTA)

The majority of technologically successful businesses will gain from the future age of the internet. Thus our honorable mention list is in no way complete. The diversity of the list, though, reveals the metaverse's second and third-order benefits.

In virtual environments, Disney (DIS) can digitize its parks and release the world's most powerful IP portfolio. Snapchat's (SNAP) augmented reality, virtual reality, and critical messaging services will seamlessly move into the metaverse.

Do we honestly believe Zoom (ZM) will stop advancing in the field of 2D video conferencing?

Twitter (TWTR) is experimenting with small transactions for content in a Web3-like approach. As a growing amount of your assets sits in the virtual vs. physical realm, cybersecurity stocks such as CrowdStrike (CRWD) and Okta (OKTA) will become significantly more relevant.

Although the metaverse has the potential to cause a stir among the FAAMG firms, the most powerful technology businesses today will lead and benefit from this shift, albeit to differing degrees.

Metaverse Investment Stocks Alternatives

Purchasing a bundle of metaverse investment stocks in an ETF is an alternative to purchasing specific metaverse stocks. Any tech-heavy ETF, like Invesco QQQ or ARKK, will offer you enough access to these names.

The Roundhill Ball Metaverse ETF (META). This is among Roundhill's six ETFs that concentrate on future investing themes, including eSports, streaming, sports betting, and a variety of other topics.

As you can see, there are several methods to become acquainted with the metaverse.

Investing Early in Web 3.0

A real metaverse, like shown in Ready Player One and Tron, might be years away. Nevertheless, Facebook and other forerunners are constantly at work establishing the basis for a future in which family, friends, employees, and others may meet and engage in shared virtual spaces that look and feel real.

We are not specifically saying virtual reality headsets or video conferencing. Individuals will require real-time services, from entertainment to business, even online. We foresee organizations as varied as Amazon, Netflix, DoorDash, and Robinhood all contributing to a virtual metaverse in the future years. Cryptocurrency miners and brokers will gain from the use of digital currency.

With this in mind, we strongly advise investors to keep a close check on this sector. This is not always easy, especially since most average investors do not have private, early-stage funds.

Take, for example, Robin Hood. Following years of conjecture, shares of the millennial-favored commission-free trading software started trading on Nasdaq. Before then, only angel investors, venture capitalists, and other qualified investors who met specified capital criteria were eligible to participate. According to BNN Bloomberg's Jon Erlichman, artists Snoop Dogg and Nas were among those who put their hard-earned money in Robinhood some years ago. The firm was valued at $62 million at the time. It is now worth $32 billion, a staggering 516-fold rise.

Only in the US can a twenty-something years old Bulgarian immigrant (Robinhood creator Vlad Tenev) build a worldwide brokerage sector disrupting app. Only in the US can two guys who spent their early life on the streets and had multiple run-ins with the law become wildly successful and affluent via their musical prowess as well as their investment choices.

During its initial public offering (IPO), Robinhood was roughly eight years old, which is slightly younger than the average age of most venture-supported digital businesses when they go public. The unfortunate reality is that most firms have opted to remain private for longer rather than cope with the (rising) mountain of laws and regulations that publicly traded firms must adhere to. And by the time firms eventually decide to go public, they might have experienced their most successful era of growth.

Small investors and households are the ones that suffer the most as a result of this. Earnings from private equity can be quite high, but most ordinary Americans do not have access to it. This tendency, thankfully, seems to be changing. According to Renaissance Capital, there have been 261 new listings in 2021, the highest of any complete year dating back to 2014. However, firms have acquired an all-time high of $94.2 billion, rising more than 20% from 2020.

What is the explanation behind this? Jay Clayton deserves credit.

Clayton was one of former President Donald Trump's top selections for a government leadership position. The former chairman of the Securities and Exchange Commission (SEC), who stepped down in December 2020, made it his aim to promote more firms to list on public markets earlier in their lifespans.

He might have done something right. Clayton expressed his dissatisfaction with the lack of market access in 2018. "If this tendency continues, the economy will be dominated by a considerably smaller set of people."

This is the Time

Cryptocurrencies, notably Bitcoin and Ethereum, are some of the most appealing early-stage investments as both are still in development and have tremendous promising prospects.

According to a survey by Crypto.com, the number of individuals who utilize cryptocurrency has surpassed 220 million for the first time. At the end of June 2021, 221 million people worldwide were involved in the cryptocurrency landscape, trading, investing, and transacting in Bitcoin, Ethereum, and other digital currencies.

In addition, the rate of adoption looks to be increasing. According to Crypto.com, cryptocurrency users doubled in four months, from 100 million to 200 million. In comparison, it took nine months to go from 65 million to 100 million users.

Private investors are not the only ones pushing adoption. Michael Saylor's MicroStrategy (possessing more than 105,000 BTC at a monetary value of $4.1 billion), Tesla (43,200 BTC/$1.5 billion), and Square (8,027 BTC/$220 million) are some of the biggest firms to acknowledge owning Bitcoin on their financial statement.

According to CoinDesk, Ethereum trade volume increased by 1,400 percent in the first half of 2021, owing primarily to institutional exposure. In the first six months, the Ethereum market increased three times faster than Bitcoin. The world's second-largest cryptocurrency by market cap surpassed Bitcoin in volume growth and price performance outperforming the S&P500 and gold.

All of these are proof that online presence and the willingness to manage online portfolios are rising. This is a great investment indicator for the metaverse.

Other Ways to Get Paid in Metaverse Creator Economy

- Virtual Avatars

In many virtual environments, having an active avatar representation provides users with a sense of self. It is a natural human desire to express oneself through personal style, including hairstyles, colors, make-up, piercings, tattoos, and other physical features to clothing and accessories. In a virtual environment, the human body and any accessories have significantly more creative potential, and the creation of avatars, skins, and accessories is a rapidly expanding field. Roblox is an example of a world featuring a person-to-person avatar and accessory marketplace.

Apart from avatars in virtual environments, there is a contemporary trend of generating and selling profile images for use on Twitter or other digital platforms. Not only are human images popular right now but so are images of other animals. The most common is the generative art style, which involves creating a set of thousands of versions of unique combination rarities by randomly mixing a set of many different body shapes and accessories/modifications. Cryptopunks and Bored Apes are two well-known examples of pfp projects that have jointly sold for huge amounts of money.

CryptoPunks have become a form of a cultural phenomenon that the cheapest punk costs 102 ETH ($391k). CryptoPunks' founder, Larva Labs, has secured an agreement with UTA to represent them in content agreements for films, games, and other projects. Punks are on the verge of evolving into ideal virtual beings. Virtual beings' creative potential is an interesting topic that will be discussed later in this section.

Avatars come in different styles, from pixel art to cartoon-style 2D to powerful 3D representation with animation abilities. Through these numerous channels, you have a leeway to show your creativity and unique expertise. The proper style will depend on where you intend to sell the avatar for use.

Using nonfungible tokens to package avatars simplifies the process of establishing and selling ownership rights. Games that are not built on the blockchain network have their marketplaces and standards.

- Virtual Products

There are numerous options for what a virtual product might be and what kinds of value it can provide to entice people to purchase it. A single item could fall under more than one category.

People buy virtual products for different reasons, including creative art pieces, collectibles, investment, memorializing and proving involvement in an event, expressing support for a movement, or just looking cool.

As with the CryptoPunks, the social standing of being an informed early adopter or a heavy purchase cost supporter of a unique release collection has become a new source of worth.

- Goods with Game Utility

Aside from just aesthetic or social value, many emerging experiences go even further in terms of utility. The Sandbox game goes beyond what Roblox or Neon District can provide by enabling games developers to create creatures with statistics and other creative elements to inhabit their space.

Virtual goods for blockchain-supported environments can likewise be packaged and sold as nonfungible tokens, although they usually come with additional world-specific limits. Virtual products interoperability between settings is a hot topic in theory, but it takes a different approach in practice. It is best to determine which virtual space you want to make for first and then look into their method.

- Creators Tools/ Creator Training

Many potential gold miners incurred losses during the Gold Rush, but those who sold picks, shovels, tents, and blue jeans (Levi Strauss) earned a decent profit.

While everybody is racing to generate content in the hopes of a hit, if you have both innovative and technical talents, you can develop tools, set up training classes, or build communities to help a large number of individuals build more efficiently. 2D/3D animation technologies are typically sophisticated, requiring substantial experience and expertise, costly, or both. It is not easy to set up a model for animation with natural articulating joints and control points. Creating more simple and purpose-driven tooling or assisting individuals in learning how to get the most out of current tools with exactly what they have to know has a business opportunity.

- Content Remastering

Many 2D avatars and profile image projects are competing for attention in an increasingly congested market. Most are opting to provide 3D-built models for usage in one or more virtual environments or games to offer their owners greater value and the chance to connect as a community.

CyberKongz has been remade as 3D voxel characters for use in the Sandbox. Digital artists are in high demand to produce classic or voxel-style 3D copies of the 2D character pictures and supporting animations. Approaching nonfungible token projects that are either going to debut with eventual 3D editions or have already debuted with the promise of a later release of 3D editions are fantastic spots to engage and use your imagination and expertise to help them advance their early concepts.

- Concerts / Live Social Events in Virtual Environments

Millions of individuals may be found online in many of the most prominent games and virtual environments. Famous musical acts have made tens of millions of dollars performing concerts in these environments.

According to Paul Tassi of Forbes, merchandise sales from Fortnite with Travis Scott totaled $20 million for the artist. That is compared to his $1.7 million one-night records for an in-person Astroworld tour and little under 40% of what he recorded earning from the $53,5 million tours.

Artists with limited fan bases can still host events in virtual environments to promote digital record sales, improved streaming, and commemorative digital merchandise. Yes, the decades-old concept of a concert T-shirt could now be realized as a nonfungible token or a game skin.

Although not directly creating and selling a digital product, roles associated with developing a digital event experience will be highly demanded. Some examples are listed below:

- Director
- Broadcast Producer
- Sound Engineer
- Artist in 3D
- VFX Artist
- Lighting Artist
- Motion Capture Actor
- Motion Graphics Designer

Virtual Beings

Virtual beings are not a novel concept. An early virtual being from the 1980s, Max Headroom, was played by a human in makeup for the live segments because the technology was not strong enough to animate a real virtual being.

However, as technology gets stronger, some artists, such as Hatsune Miku, have performed at system-generated concerts in front of fans worldwide for many years. With the seeds already planted, improvements in visual fidelity and artificial intelligence to increase lifelike action have changed in the last several years. At times, artificial intelligence is even dictating what the virtual being says.

The founder of Virtual Influencer Agency, Dudley Neville-Spencer, uses social listening and artificial intelligence to closely match characters, speech patterns, and the target demographic.

Virtual beings have taken on the roles of social media influencers and artists, fashion models, cause campaigners, and others. Lil Miquela alone nailed all of them, and there are plenty more virtual beings.

5

CHALLENGES AND REQUIREMENTS OF METAVERSE

Challenges of the Metaverse

Till now, we don't have a clear idea of what the metaverse space will look like, but we can expect it to face the following challenges to become a full functioning virtual environment:

- Reputation and Identity in the Metaverse

When we speak of the physical world, the issue of personal identification and representation is quite easy. However, when it comes to virtual worlds or the metaverse, one can question what exactly constitutes one's identity. And, most importantly, how to show that you are who you say you are, rather than someone or a robot attempting to simulate your identity. This is where reputation comes into play, not only in identification but also in verifying that the party with which one interacts is reputable and legitimate. The ability to manufacture facial characteristics, footage, and voice pose the greatest obstacle. Therefore, we can expect new identification methods to emerge in the coming years.

- Data and Security in Metaverse

Although businesses and organizations continue to improve their internet security systems, data protection has long been an issue for individuals in many online spaces. Delving deep into the metaverse will necessitate the evolution of security systems to a whole new level to keep up with the metaverse's ever-expanding environment. This would necessitate the development of new personal data and data protection systems to ensure the security of one's identity and belongings in the virtual environment. As a result, personal identification may reach a stage where participants must supply more personal information than is now required to identify themselves and verify that the security system functions properly, keeping personal information safe.

- Metaverse's Currency and Payment Systems

Bitcoin is one of the most popular examples of digital currency, which has been around for several years. The same can be said for online markets such as Amazon and eBay, which link millions of people worldwide. Without a doubt, metaverse would have its online marketplace, integrating several physical and digital currencies for quick and easy trading. It will be particularly important to build a unique new transaction validation mechanism, irrespective of the currency or marketplace structure when it comes to transactions. The challenge will be persuading participants that they can trust and, more importantly, feel safe when trading in the metaverse space.

- Law and Jurisdiction in Metaverse

Identifying jurisdiction and laws that can guarantee the virtual environment is safe and protected for its users will be a major task. The subject of law and jurisdiction will arise due to countries' immersion in the metaverse, necessitating a greater focus on virtual legal areas. With the rising virtual world available to people worldwide, it will be necessary to determine how the jurisdiction will be applied. The metaverse is poised to attract a huge number of people together, making it a terrific platform to interact and exchange information. Still, it also puts participants at risk if no regulations govern the boundaries.

- Ownership and Property in Metaverse

When we talk about a single integrated virtual environment where you can connect with the world and other people, just like in the physical world, we may envisage buying and selling different products and assets. NFTs have accelerated their rise to prominence, creating waves in 2021 and drawing more investors and consumers to digital assets and tokens. The task will be to create a uniform platform that can authenticate the owners of digital assets in the metaverse, comparable to how nonfungible tokens already depict physical-world items, providing and verifying ownership rights for artwork, music, films and much more.

Virtual real estate agencies? (handwritten note in margin)

- Metaverse's Community and Network

Without question, metaverse space will unite a varied group of people together, bringing individuals from all over the world together in a single virtual reality. As the past couple of years have demonstrated, being interconnected is a necessity for people, resulting in forming a powerful network in the metaverse for business and personal reasons. Metaverse has the potential to become a technology for several people to connect and build genuine relationships. We are used to talking via the internet, but for the metaverse to become a place where users can feel mentally and physically present, haptic and motion capture innovation will need to progress to a whole different level. This level will allow for a great understanding of one's existence and environment and visual fidelity, and the capacity to touch and feel.

- Time and Space in Metaverse

When comparing the physical world to a virtual world, the idea of time perception can be varied, as participants seem to be less aware of their bodies while within the VR. People may subconsciously devote considerable time within the metaverse as a result of the full interaction.

Given the risk of a skewed sense of time, it is critical to implement systems that keep participants in touch with reality. The concept of space is another concept worth considering in the metaverse world. Because the metaverse implies an unlimited space, it may be difficult for participants to submerge themselves in such a massive world at first, trying to absorb the volume and myriad of information available all at once. To guarantee participants are both aware and secure while within the virtual world, both time and space interpretation in the metaverse will need direction during the first phases of immersion.

And although we are still on the verge of creating a virtual world, setting up the metaverse might be both difficult and rewarding. It is unquestionably necessary to ensure that the metaverse serves as a supplement to the physical world we live in rather than a replacement for. As exciting as the virtual world is, it is critical to be informed, protected, and secure in this new huge environment.

Potential Legal Issues

When it comes to digital activities, there is a chance of practicing "fraud." One who deliberately deceives someone to convince him to modify his position to his detriment is liable for any damage he receives.

However, the conduct of fraudulent transactions may be increasingly difficult with the arrival of these advanced technologies. The criminals, on the other hand, always devise a method to profit from the technical flaws. In principle, the law lags behind technology, and this will very certainly continue indefinitely. This is the case because technology progresses at a breakneck pace, and the law usually follows suit. The legal system develops new laws by issuing court judgments at the administrative, state, and federal levels. In most circumstances, the legislative body prepares and promulgates bills as a reactionary step. Most, if not all, laws were introduced and passed in response to serious concerns like cyberstalking, cyberbullying, revenge porn, kidnapping, or child pornography.

In the virtual space, there is also the possibility of "stealing" or "conversion." We should not be fooled into believing that we cannot lose money or possessions simply because we are in the so-called digital age. When a victim's finances or assets are taken without their agreement, this is referred to as theft in civil courts. In the metaverse, there is likely less of a probability of committing theft now. Nevertheless, we are convinced that the criminals will find a method to escape.

Requirements for Future Metaverse

There is a lot of anticipation for the future of the metaverse! However, there is still more work to make it a reality for people, companies, brands, and communities. Several essential aspects must be considered to create a vibrant and flourishing metaverse that provides advantages and opportunities to the greatest number of people.

- Next Wave Digitization

Since the 1990s, there has been a considerable surge in digitization. The first 2G cellular network was launched in 1991, and decades after, 5G networks increased digitally. More of our events, settings, and things will need to be swiftly digitized in many and varied media forms due to these improvements.

The digital twin is a concept used to denote both digitized and born-digital content. A rise in the digitalization of historical components is also necessary for the metaverse to capture not only creation in our changing present and future culture. This need is driven by the desire to deliver content, goods, and services to clients on-demand and anywhere they can access the internet at a low cost.

Companies that have not undergone a significant digital transformation in all elements of their culture, staff, goods, activities, and services risk becoming irrelevant, obsolescent, or even extinct. The time has come for a company to start investing in introducing its goods and services to digital marketplaces. With radical shift and reprioritization, it is still possible to meet up and engage in the metaverse.

- Interoperability and portability

Avatars, 3D models, AR, VR, MR, XR, and spatial settings are just a few of the asset types that are fast evolving due to market innovation. Asset classes combine with information to create content bundles that fill the metaverse's numerous platforms. Most of these technologies are likely to be exclusive or platform-dependent. While these platform-specific and private methodologies may rapidly expand innovation, the metaverse will necessitate product and content portability and interoperability across platforms.

Published and open documentation, continual traveling unique identifiers, direct asset transfer from one platform to another without extensive third-party services, and shared portability, which allows groups of participants to communicate and interact together, are all important elements of portability.

Interoperability allows assets and data to be shared across platforms and networks. There are various principles, but they do not yet account for all of the new media kinds that exist now in a comprehensive and integrated fashion, much alone equip us with asset and data types that may emerge in the future. Existing standards also do not cater to massive amounts of unstructured data. It also fails to account for digital assets of various sorts using minimally feasible and simple techniques.

There is no shared data framework for the metaverse space, and there is not even one for current systems. However, if accepted by others in an enlarged transparent landscape, an improved shared data framework, like the one created by Microsoft, might figure out the next step toward a more comprehensive approach to data and metadata. More devoted collaboration and cooperation across the business, government, and nonprofit players, like with the Open Data Initiative in the past, must be promoted to produce open standards quickly. The metaverse must be cross-platform to be available to as many individuals as possible. It must function fluidly across partners and platforms.

- Migration, Emulation, and Representation

Assets and data must be handled continually during their lifetime from source software and hardware ecosystems into new ones as technology continually develops for a healthy metaverse to thrive with the complexity of the digitized and born-digital present and future. Emulation, migration, and representation will create a metaverse full of a range of history and modern creativity.

Emulation attempts to replicate the content's experience and appearance in its original context while allowing for technical modifications in the background. Assets and data are moved into new settings and landscapes, often with major modifications in conditions or experience, generating meaning and interpretation that differs significantly from the source.

The sense of assets and data evolving and moving across the metaverse in newer media, styles, and platforms are known as re-presentation. It is crucial to consider data and assets and the metaverse itself as performative regarding what occurs in a computational setting and what activities and interactions people have.

- Copyright at the Pace of Innovation

Copyright might be a serious stumbling block to the metaverse's expansion and reasonable use. The basic norm regarding copyright protection in the US for works established after January 1, 1978, is that it lasts for the author's lifetime plus an extra 70 years. Even the US Congress's copyright legislation of 1790, which provided for 14 years of protection, could be too lengthy.

While a specific intellectual property may have long-term value for its creators, the pace of creation and copyright framework does not always function in the metaverse, given the huge amount of information made with freely available and flexible digital tools. Many experts in the metaverse are users who customize things to meet their own demands. These users are referred to as prosumers. It is the prosumers' abilities

✱ *Prosumers*

and dispositions to remix and remake digital assets and data scale knowledge, brand strength, and market expansion in a digital culture.

Content in the metaverse requires substantially shorter copyright periods that change at the pace of innovation generated by digital content development, with lifespans ranging from minutes to less than two years. Clear, unambiguous, and worldwide rights to use and reuse content that fosters creativity while sustaining artists and rewarding new content development are critical, particularly as human and machine manufacturers create the metaverse.

With cloud computing's vast resources, computers may occasionally generate new content nearly instantly. Furthermore, certain governments may impose additional restrictions on free worldwide commerce, such as legacy and moral rights, which hinder the freedom of artists and creators with the desire and means to collaborate and create globally across people, places, and goods via the internet. More international collaboration among many players will be required to build a copyright system and licensing systems that move at the pace of innovation, just as it will be required for interoperability and portability.

- Global Commons of the Metaverse

The metaverse may also require a new global commons based on a globally operating system such as Creative Commons legal tools, both human and computer friendly. A commons, or a collection of shared resources that everyone may add to and take from, is critical in the metaverse's connection with marketplaces as a driver of ideas. Individual artists, companies, and communities will all have to agree to unified policies and vital financial support for the metaverse's commons. A commons is a gathering space where we may share, cooperate, and collaborate.

At the same time, the metaverse's global commons must be a springboard of possibilities that allows for self-expression, identity, and expandable prospects for self-actualization. A viable global commons in the metaverse will need dialogue, judgment, compassion, and trust to be effective. The metaverse will be built upon open access. The Creative Commons Attribution license and Creative Commons Zero Public Domain Dedication are the legal instruments better placed to facilitate open Access in the world metaverse at this moment since they permit economic reuse, remixing, distribution, and new content development.

Crucible Networks, Outlier Ventures, and the Open Metaverse Interoperability Group are organizations and entities working to develop an open metaverse. Crucible Networks' goal is to establish "open metaverse architecture" by developing common standards that enable individuals to utilize the same avatar and digital identities across mediums. The Open Metaverse OS was designed by Outlier Ventures. It is a decentralized OS based on Decentralized Finance, nonfungible tokens, and crypto. Finally, the Open Metaverse Interoperability Group explores interoperable identities and designs standards for social networks and inventories to bridge virtual environments.

- Standards Required

Whether it is referred to as the spatial web or the metaverse, the technology will require standards. IEEE and the Spatial Web Foundation have declared partnerships and support for full standards to allow legally-aligned 21st Century "cyber-physical" web. Since the spatial web is the next phase of global network technology, this is a significant step forward. The spatial web will unleash smart Cities and the metaverse. An ultra-connected, contextually conscious network of people, artificial intelligence, and computers will enable the creation of digital twins, as well as other forms of digitalization.

This collaboration set of metaverse standards was produced not simply by developers but also by privacy activists, technology experts, and cybersecurity specialists. Hyperspatial Domains, Hyperspatial Transaction Protocol (HSTP), and Hyperspatial Modeling Language (HSML) are among the spatial web Foundation requirements that regulate   context-conscious collaborative technology   that guarantees data authenticity data lineage, and data interoperability across integrated hardware.

The XR Safety Initiative (XRSI) has also created a collection of standard definitions for the extended reality space (an umbrella term for all interactive systems, including augmented reality and virtual reality) and a new collection of standards for diversity inclusion ethics, and safety. XRSI recently published a concept for privacy and safety in extended reality and is now working on version 1.1, which will broaden the scope to include the metaverse. Furthermore, this non-profit is counseling several United States lawmakers and senators on security, privacy, and trust for extremely sensitive sectors like Immersive Healthcare. They are also collaborating with the Australian eSafety Commissioner and the British National Health Service.

- The Importance of Sustainability

The enthusiasm for the metaverse should be matched by efforts to ensure its commercial and environmental viability. The materials used to design the metaverse systems should ideally be built from recyclable or biodegradable materials. The capacity to change and repair gadgets will be critical in enabling more individuals worldwide to engage in the metaverse. Due to climate, public health, and safety concerns, the resources, and production capacity will substantially influence users within their locations.

To improve and enhance our interlinked suite of gadgets in the metaverse, we must learn both soft and hard technological abilities. Hardware and software will have to be durable to last long enough to enable several people to join the industry with their tools. The metaverse must be built with a genuine effort to handle climate change, pollution, waste, and aftermath effects. All persons participating in the creation of the real world and the metaverse must practice long-term sustainability.

- Design that is both Accessible and Inclusive

The metaverse should make assets, data, and platforms available to serve a wide spectrum of consumers. Diverse groups of individuals, including those with impairments, benefit from inclusive design techniques. In terms of accessibility, the metaverse should not fall into the failures of the past. It is critical to incorporate accessibility into the metaverse's underlying technology, apps, and rules. Accessibility is a prerequisite for the emergence of the metaverse. The metaverse will profit by collaborating with and learning from people with diverse needs and viewpoints. People, corporations, and communities whose lived experiences and substantial knowledge define routes ahead will steer an accessible and inclusive metaverse. Like the other elements addressed in this section, global collaboration and shared resources are critical for success.

@ Nat — Add voice to fortunes?

6

NEW PROJECTS AND OPPORTUNITIES: A CASE OF FACEBOOK

Recently, Zuckerberg presented social VR with Horizon Home, which employs an Oculus Quest 2 virtual reality headset as part of a larger initiative. He also hinted the release of new AR glasses (Nazare) and a high-end virtual reality headset (Project Cambria) in the nearest future. We have summarized below a list of ongoing and future collaborations and projects by Facebook for the continuity of metaverse.

Facebook Product and Project Collaboration

Games

According to Mark Zuckerberg, games will be prevalent in the metaverse. Facebook has teamed up with Vertigo Games, a virtual reality gaming firm, on five forthcoming releases. Zuckerberg applauded Beat Saber, which just surpassed $100 million in sales on Quest alone. Since its release last year, Population: One, a battle royale shooter on Quest, has been the most popular virtual reality multiplayer shooter game on the platform.

Following the recent release of Resident Evil 4 on the Quest, Grand Theft Auto: San Andreas is also heading to virtual reality. Later this year, Quest will release Blade & Sorcery: Nomad. It was a fresh version of one of the finest games ever developed. There is a wide variety of concepts on metaverse, including a simple game of chess played with a buddy through AR, fencing with a distant partner, and even playing basketball against pals via virtual reality.

XR Fitness

Supernatural boxing and new FitXR workout classes are among the new fitness activities on Oculus. Guided and hand-tracked bodyweight workouts have been included in Player 22 by Rezzil, which professional athletes now utilize.

Facebook will equally launch Active Pack for Quest 2 in 2022. The company is working on a fitness accessory pack for Quest 2 that includes controller grips for when stuff gets heated and a facial interface that can be wiped clean to make your experiences more enjoyable.

You will be able to work out with an AI in new environments. You will be able to play fitness games in groups, such as three-on-three basketball. Quest for business, which includes Work Accounts support for Quest 2, was also launched by Facebook. The new business offering will add work features to Quest devices for consumers, such as the option to log into Quest 2 using a Work Account rather than your individual Facebook account. Account management, IDP & SSO integration, mobile device management, and more technologies will be available to enterprises.

Horizon Home will also have 2D applications for Quest. Slack, Dropbox, Facebook, Instagram, and other services will soon operate in virtual reality as 2D panel applications in Horizon Home, allowing you to multitask, tick items off your to-do list between game sessions, and stay connected while in virtual reality. This kicks off the metaverse integration of some of your preferred 2D internet services.

Horizon Home now includes a new customized workspace environment from Facebook. This is an area where you can concentrate and work with the new 2D panel apps or cross items off your to-do list.

Working in the metaverse, with technologies like teleportation, might save the environment a lot of money if you take one less business trip per year.

Oculus Developers

Facebook is announcing its Presence Platform on the Quest platform, which includes different machine perception and artificial intelligence features that will enable developers to create MR experiences. Presence Platform's features, including contextual awareness, content placement and persistence, voice interaction, and standardized hand interactions, deliver on this promise, allowing users to feel submerged in the metaverse.

The Presence Platform includes three products: the Insight software development kit (SDK) for creating MR experiences, the Interaction SDK for adding hand interactions to applications, and the Voice SDK for incorporating voice input into the experiences they create.

It also releases tools to let developers create and test progressive web applications (PWA) on Quest devices. Developers will be able to send their PWAs to App Lab in the nearest future.

Developers of PWAs will submit application packages to Oculus, and their applications will appear in the Oculus Store or Application Lab. Because PWA applications display live content from the creators' site, they do not require application package upgrades. This will enable developers to turn their site's 2D experience into an Oculus application.

The Avatars 2.0 SDK, which overhauls Avatars in virtual reality, will be released soon. Also, Facebook will unveil a new cloud backup system that will allow individuals to back up their device's application data, such as game progress or settings, so they can instantly resume where they left off in a game. It operates at the filesystem level and does not require any code. Facebook has stated that it is experimenting with new ways of perceiving ownership, like NFTs.

Multiplayer gameplay will also be improved. To assist developers began with the new social platform APIs, Facebook created a new multiplayer example called SharedSpaces. This offers direct invite application programming interfaces (APIs), which allow you to issue invites from your user interface. It will also provide a new channel known as Ask to Join into an application from discovery surfaces and new ways to buddy other users and find possibilities in virtual reality and 2D. It is compatible with both Unity and Unreal 4.

AR

Facebook plans to spend a huge amount of money on the basic technology and engineering required to bring fully-featured glasses to market as virtual reality reaches a tipping point.

With Ray-Ban Stories, the business claims to have put as much technology as possible into good-looking spectacles; it is also working on fully-fledged augmented reality glasses. The Spark AR platform claims to build content, capabilities, and communities that may enhance Facebook experiences while also illuminating the route to AR glasses in the future.

Facebook is seeing many more people engage with augmented reality technology today thanks to Spark AR, Facebook's AR platform for creation and distribution across applications and devices. Every month, Facebook claims that over 700 million users utilize augmented effects across its applications and devices.

New Spark AR features will open more advanced AR experiences and applications with location services, virtual objects, and new input models. It has new geo-locked public-space experiences. Using several augmented reality activation sites enables location-locked effects that connect in a coherent, long-form experience. Consider a treasure hunt at a theme park or a guided tour of landmarks in a city center. Spark AR is now in beta with the Spark Partner Network and a few chosen businesses, like Sanrio in Japan, before being made available to all developers in 2022.

Social VR

Facebook announced Horizon Home. When you attend an Oculus Party in virtual reality, you will soon be able to bring your pals into a modern social version of your home, wherein their avatars will be embodied. You will be able to hang out with friends, view movies with them, and play games and applications.

Plus, with Messenger calling in virtual reality in the pipeline, you will be able to interact with your pals across all of your applications and devices. You will be able to ask your Facebook friends to join a Messenger call wherever in virtual reality, and you will be able to have fun together.

Horizon Home, Horizon Workroom, and Horizon Worlds are all part of the company's mission to build virtual reality settings for the home, office, and other environments.

Facebook Horizon

Facebook Horizon is a VR social network. It is a tool for creating sandboxes for social interaction in which participants can interact with a virtual world. It will be a unique and huge multiplayer virtual reality game. Horizon allows you to design your unique digital avatars and travel across virtual worlds through Telepods. Telepods are magical portals that transfer you to various lobbies where you may play games and watch shows.

You may also enjoy movies, listen to music, and play multiplayer games with your buddies. Horizon will include real guides called Horizon Locals. These real guides aid users and ensure their safety in the virtual environment.

Workrooms

Workrooms are virtual meeting area that allows you and your coworkers to collaborate more effectively from any location. You may join a conference in virtual reality as an avatar or make a video call from the PC to the virtual room. You may collaborate on ideas using a large virtual board, bring your computer and keyboard into virtual reality to collaborate with others, or have immersive discussions that seem more like you are in person.

Features of Workrooms

- Bring your space, pc, and keyboard with you into virtual reality

Working in virtual reality does not imply you have to abandon your usual tools. Workrooms are an MR experience that allows you to transport your real workspace and tracked keyboard into the virtual room and experience them in the virtual conference in front of you. You may take some notes in presentations, bring files into virtual reality, and even share your screen with coworkers if you want to.

Follow up

- Experience a real-world space with avatars and spatial audio

With the new and enhanced Oculus Avatars and spatial audio technologies, you will feel more connected in an immersive experience. The avatars provide a wide range of customization possibilities and are more immersive, allowing you to feel as if you are truly there with your coworkers. With the high-quality, low-latency spatial audio, you will hear the individuals around you, much as they would in a real room, allowing discussions to flow effortlessly.

- A virtual whiteboard the size of your thoughts

Every area in Workrooms has an unlimited whiteboard so you can collaborate on ideas in real-time. You can turn the controller around and use it to write, either on the actual desk in front of you or while standing by the whiteboard. You may equally use the whiteboard to pin photos from your pc, which you can subsequently mark up and discuss with others. Workrooms save your whiteboards for the period you need them, so you may return at any moment and keep working from the same location.

- A room to fit every task

You may change the arrangement of the virtual space to suit your needs. There is a seating plan for any occasion, and the entire space adjusts up and down to accommodate the size of your group, whether you are focusing on cooperation, discussion, or presentation.

- Join in virtual reality or by video call

Because not everyone has a virtual reality headset, you may also join a room via video call through the computer. By simply posting a meeting link, you may invite visitors to join the call. Like in a real meeting room, video users will appear on a video screen in the virtual space. You can handle up to 16 individuals in virtual reality at once and up to 50 persons on a call in total, including video users.

- Designed to use your hand

This allows you to transition more readily between physical tools such as the keyboard and controllers as required, resulting in a more fluid and immersive social experience.

Body Tracking and Hand Tracking

Through augmented reality effects, Facebook will enable "more fanciful, entertaining, and inventive self-expression," according to the company. It is laying the groundwork for people-centric types of input and virtual object interaction in AR.

The new Virtual Objects Pipeline, according to the business, would allow users to create and deploy 3D objects in the physical world, including text, characters, GIFs, stickers, and more. This will also contain core technological capabilities such as depth, occlusion, and enhanced plane tracking to ensure realistic performance.

Virtual items are important to the future of augmented reality and the metaverse's development. These objects, constructed on Spark AR, will be adaptable and scalable over diverse surfaces and applications such as commerce and retail and include virtual try-ons and product previews.

Facebook claims to be making it simpler for producers to engage in the AR environment and reach more audiences. Polar is the business's new, free iOS app that, according to the company, makes it simple to envision, create, and share augmented reality effects and filters without having to write or use the Spark AR Studio. Creators will expand their brands, art, and creative vision in new ways, such as a virtual sticker with their catchphrase or swag to offer during an AMA.

Facebook also announced that its Facebook Reality Labs would invest $150 million in an education initiative focused on helping AR/VR artists and developers generate economic opportunities, including new training and career development resources as well as new content and technology collaborations.

Facebook is extending the Spark AR Curriculum to include more AR training courses, including a new "AR Pro" course, as well as an official Spark AR certification program, after over 22,000 artists registered in the AR Curriculum program in less than a year.

Spark AR Certification

For the first time, Facebook will offer augmented reality developers a structured path and program to show their understanding and competency with Spark AR and receive the Facebook Certified Spark AR Creator certificate.

The Facebook Certification Career Network will be available to creators who acquire the Spark AR Certification. Facebook is also partnering with Unity, a game engine developer, to enable individuals to learn how to make fantastic virtual reality content by combining Unity's "Create with VR for Educators" tool and training with Quest 2 devices for organizations and educational institutions.

7

FUTURE OF METAVERSE

Discussions about the metaverse are becoming increasingly popular. It is most likely since big tech companies like Microsoft and Facebook believe it is time to go all-in on metaverse, leading you to believe it will be the next big thing after artificial intelligence.

The metaverse's meaning is continuously growing. As our physical world, humanity is still in the dark regarding most of its mysteries, and we are on the verge of discovering them. AR and VR are just the tips of the iceberg.

Cryptocurrency

Cryptocurrencies will be used to facilitate trade inside the metaverse. This might originate from Bitcoin, Ethereum, or Cardano, but new cryptocurrencies are constantly being developed. The end outcome will be a metaverse-created digital item that can be safeguarded and sold utilizing blockchain and NFT technology. This implies that the metaverse will develop an economy comparable to that of the real world.

A cryptocurrency that can travel between the physical world and the metaverse will surely raise the stakes and drive many new companies.

The big virtual natives will most certainly develop their own Milky Way (or perhaps galaxy) in the metaverse, where small businesses may be developing the equivalent of little planets in which you can enjoy yourself if you have the funds. However, like the Internet in the early 1990s, the metaverse will have to mature first. Based on the early buzz, it is expected that augmented reality and virtual reality initiatives will be the most common.

Gaming firms, such as Epic Games, which is pushing the limits with Fortnite and hosting events such as digital concerts, are clear players to flourish in the early phases. E-commerce and small businesses will soon join the trend, but business-to-consumer businesses will not be the only ones attempting to figure out how to take advantage of the metaverse; the business-to-business sector also has a lot to gain.

Prospect

The metaverse's potential to capture data from its environments, including the biosphere, will determine whether it succeeds or fails. The only way to do so will be to absorb large amounts of data from IoT. Only with this data can you build a rich and genuine world. After "seeing" the following requirement, the next requirement will be "interacting," which means that the data need not only be meaningfully displayed but must also be responsive.

On the most basic level, you may picture the demands of a digital design in the metaverse, which are similar to the fundamental needs of humans in the physical world: tools for data intake and access, as well as the design to store, analyze, and enrich data. However, just like in the physical world, security must be ensured before any significant transactions occur.

With all of the focus on the metaverse's fascinating prospects, it is easy to overlook the infrastructure required to carry out the heavy lifting. Not only would historical data be present to provide meaning and dimension in any interaction, but it will also need to be extremely accurate to make the metaverse appealing. It would need to be optimized for data retrieval and storage. This necessitates the requirement for real-time data intake and analytics. Major technology stack advancements will be required in addition to significant infrastructure innovations.

(handwritten margin note: followup — invest?)

Event-driven World

The metaverse must be event-driven, meaning that any important change in the state must be signaled and reacted to by the interested audience to be in line with the physical world.

Furthermore, semantics, along with context, will be vitally crucial. You understand the purpose of that data and establish the meaning of it at the time it is saved in a segregated world where you own your data. Data in the metaverse, on the other hand, is expected to be widely dispersed. In a world where you rely on your environment for data, understanding the meaning of the data shared with you is critical. A lingua franca may be required to evaluate formats and measurements accurately.

On the internet, security and trust are critical. Presently, the most common method of addressing Internet trust is through restricted access. We are used to websites being "partitioned," with distinct clickwrap or browsewrap terms of service. Because this method does not lend itself to seamlessness in the metaverse, a technological solution would be required, such as decentralized smart contracts on a metaverse. This, together with certain difficult lessons on safeguarding data in technological infrastructure, may enable the metaverse to implement protections with minimum impact.

The metaverse will not be generated with a big bang, according to popular belief. Still, once the foundation is built, it will open up a whole new world of possibilities and limitless creation. Users will gravitate to the metaverse for gaming and entertainment. At the same time, firms will likely experiment with VR meetings to improve business collaboration and take training to the next level with a completely simulated world.

The metaverse, which has long been seen as a futuristic fantasy, is rapidly becoming a reality.

Future Opportunities

Experts predict that the metaverse space will profoundly impact the world as a whole, besides just our professions and daily lives. In a statement, Yat Siu, co-founder and chairman of Animoca Brands, said, "The metaverse will come like a digital country or possibly a whole new civilization." According to Eric Elliot, creator of DevAnywhere, the metaverse can grow to be a worldwide technology worth ten times the existing global economy's value.

Below is a quick rundown of different ways the metaverse can impact our lives in the future:

- Staff will not be captured on camera without their trousers on.

The famous video of a reporter captured on camera without trousers was one of the headlines of the COVID-19 pandemic. There is less tendency of accidents in a virtual environment when you can construct a 'fully clothed' avatar.

Facebook's virtual reality platform Horizon Workrooms, an online meeting area for remote employees, is an example of VR and MR technology expanding beyond the physical world. Its goal is to build an interactive virtual world in which users' avatars may interact with one another and offer functionality that real people desire to use, which could lead to zero rent for firms.

During the COVID-19 epidemic, we experienced the cause-and-effect relationship in action. Staff working from home resulted in higher earnings for many organizations that already had their digital systems in place.

- Transformation of the concept of Homeschooling

Another significant development that occurred during the crisis was in the field of education. Most children were compelled to study from home as schools around the world closed their doors during the numerous restrictions, and some even later, to limit the chance of the virus spreading.

This compelled schools and the education sector as a whole to devise new methods of communication, collaboration, and evaluation. The number of technologies needed to stay productive increased dramatically.

Classrooms can be modified in the same way that workplaces in the metaverse can be made more interactive. It has the potential to encourage greater social interactions and eliminate the grids of melancholy faces that can be seen during video chats. Learning might even be turned into a game.

Kwang Hyung Lee of the Korean Advanced Institute of Science and Technology (KAIST) believes that academic institutions with the finest digital technologies and internet knowledgeable human resources will arise as the frontrunners, just as decentralized finance (DeFi) is set to destabilize the current traditional financial institution.

- Play to earn

Players of games such as Roblox and Minecraft have already spent considerable time inventing and creating an environment to play. Leisure mobile gaming has become more popular, with games such as Ludo helping bridge the generation gap. Candy Crush, PUBG, and Clan Wars are among the most popular games among smartphone users.

Players are flocking to MIR4's platform for the potential to earn cryptocurrencies, even though the game received mainly negative reviews. And though they may gain in-game monetary tokens, they are rarely exchangeable for real money or usable outside of the game. 'Play to Earn' is an idea that tries to change that. Players in Southeast Asia are now benefiting from platforms such as Axie Infinity by supplementing their income with their revenue.

More sophisticated blockchain-based projects, such as The Sandbox

+ Sandbox

and Decentraland, go even further by enabling players to generate their own NFTs and sell them to other participants, similar to Roblox and Minecraft. Because these transactions are conducted through Ether, the earnings can be converted into fiat currency or another crypto for usage in the physical world.

- Online shopping

Online shopping is now pretty easy, with sites like Amazon and Flipkart providing quick delivery and diverse products. Nevertheless, difficulties such as proper fitting, glitches in the refund procedure, and the ability to see what a certain item could appear like in real life remain unresolved – particularly when it comes to clothing material.

Lenskart, an Indian eyeglasses e-commerce startup, has made efforts toward virtual tryouts by showing how several glasses frames would appear on you using a video camera. Furthermore, you will not be buying solely for yourself. New virtual fashion ideas and avatar 'skins' will arise, paving the way for fashion houses and companies to thrive solely online.

Virtual tryouts may become ever more crucial as people's work hours shift, making getting the perfect tie for your avatar in the metaverse is much more vital.

- Tourism and travel

Due to travel restrictions last year, virtual reality tours of ancient Greece and Egypt were trendy. On the other hand, creators of the metaverse hope to submerge users and re-enact historical events like the American Civil War. Therefore, not only will you have the chance to cross borders without leaving your home, you will likewise be able to travel back in time.

Tourist metaverse applications using MR are being developed to direct drivers, provide additional information about landmarks they are viewing, and connect people for more delightful interactions. A visitor to a museum, for instance, could instantly receive more context or facts about the objects they are viewing.

Furthermore, because offices are embracing the metaverse for collaboration, as previously noted, there is less tendency to travel long distances, saving money and fuel. Students who desire to study at overseas colleges will save a lot of money because their need for housing and travel will be eliminated.

- Attending concerts and partying online

Houseparty, Netflix Party, Eventbrite, and Twitter variety of new features to enable greater video experiences between people during the last pandemic are just a few of the platforms that aimed to improve how people may party online even if they are trapped at home during the multiple lockdowns.

It is a lot comfortable than going out and partying in real life. It does, although, lack the "physical sense" of a real-life party. The metaverse is attempting to close the gap. Participants can now buy land, own properties, and host any events they want, thanks to initiatives such as The Sandbox, built on the Ethereum blockchain network. Snoop Dogg, the rapper, has already rebuilt his house in The Sandbox metaverse and is offering users VIP tickets to his event.

- Online digital property ownership

Investors have been drawn to artworks and parcels of land in the real world. Would you be astonished to learn about large estates made up entirely of virtual property holdings purchased online?

As a larger portion of the population becomes involved in the metaverse space, at least a few individuals have recognized the significance of 'land' in a digital environment. Land is a type of NFT, and investors have flocked to Decentraland, Sandbox, and Cryptovoxels to purchase them.

- In search of adventure as a means of escaping reality

Unless one is James Bond, the physical world is somewhat limited.

How else do you explain the never-ending search for adrenaline-pumping theme parks, skydiving, adventurous cuisine, and virtual worlds?

As virtual reality advances in the metaverse space, even people who are not billionaires will be able to participate in exciting activities. For instance, ten pals who live far apart can go boating, biking, mountain climbing, diving, roller-coaster riding, or even journey to space.

Many game players have already experienced how fantastic it can be - products such as Second Life, EVE Online, and Minecraft have conditioned participants to believe that a wholly virtual environment can replicate experiences, have a functioning civilization, and provide economies of scale.

- Changing our computer interactions

This might affect daily life, similar to how touchscreens have existed for many years but only became popular with the iPhone. If VR hardware becomes more widely available due to the metaverse, we might consider it more normal to wave our fingers in the air and expect computers to respond.

- It is all connected to decentralized finance.

The traditional banking industry is absent from the metaverse. Instead, cryptocurrency-based decentralized finance (DeFi) solutions are gaining traction in the metaverse space. It is how nonfungible tokens and digital assets are purchased, tickets are sold, one token is traded for another, and other transactions are carried out.

If traditional banks remain missing, the momentum of individuals living in the metaverse grows. Decentralized Finance will explode simply due to the increase in the volume of transactions. Every metaverse network has attempted to employ a separate cryptocurrency so far. Diem, Facebook's stablecoin, may unite the metaverse.

- The technology you buy will change as a result of the metaverse.

The metaverse, like its applications, is multifaceted. Much as getting a keyboard and mouse is common when buying a personal computer, incorporating the metaverse into our life may modify the technology we need to thrive in the virtual environment.

At the lower end, apps may be able to access the metaverse just by employing a simple camera, like the one that comes with any laptop or phone. This would allow them to work in mixed-reality mode. Your screen shows the camera's physical environment but with a transparent layer added by the application — similar to Pokémon GO's user interface.

The most creative and extensive metaverse applications employ a virtual reality headset from a firm such as Oculus. To operate a virtual reality headset smoothly, you need a high-end smartphone or a strong laptop or desktop computer with a solid graphics card and processor. While a virtual reality headset is difficult to use while moving around — a boon for firms wanting to prevent staff from playing around during working from home — but may provide the most interactive experience.

The Metaverse is Evolving

According to Vlad Panchenko, CEO and Founder of DMarket, a marketplace, and platform for creating virtual environments, today's metaverses are simplified virtual objects or virtual services available with or without virtual reality headsets.

According to Panchenko, the future metaverse includes:

- Ubiquitous networking
- Blockchain with Nonfungible Tokens
- Extended Reality (XR) with VR, AR, and MR.
- And possibly other newer technology

Furthermore, according to him, metaverse will develop into the omniverse with many cross-chain potentials. The virtual economy will equate to the physical economy in importance. Several businesses are migrating towards the metaverse, either by accident or on purpose, resulting in a global economy that will outperform the existing one many times over. There will be no choice but to participate. Otherwise, as a brand, you would not survive.

Gaming, crypto, fashion, and Hollywood are some of the businesses that were the first to develop metaverses. In addition, more clothing companies and celebrities are becoming involved in gaming metaverses. The recent examples are Gucci and Roblox firms. According to a Roblox announcement, the House brought many rare products to the platform last year with the help of their creator community. They are now happy to announce the next step of their brand as Gucci joins the metaverse in a novel, and interesting way. A digital Gucci Garden environment was open to everybody on Roblox for two weeks at the end of May, coinciding with the House's Gucci Garden Archetypes launch — an interactive audiovisual creation in Florence, Italy that examines and embraces the house's distinctive creative vision. Gucci also released a unique edition of digital bags in the game that sold for $4,115 (350.000 Robux, the game's native coin), higher than the retail price of $3,400.

Knowledge Businesses Require

According to Panchenko, designing a strategy for transferring your business into the virtual environment is critical and prepares your brand for the metaverse. In a few years to come, the metaverse will have millions of employment and thousands of brands. Those who prepare today will have a share of tomorrow's multi-trillion-dollar economy."

Christian Velitchkov, a co-founder of the digital marketing agency Twiz.io, says that creating a participant-driven interaction design that encompasses completely immersive digital experiences is what it takes to establish a metaverse around your business these days. It is also about creating a design that allows seasoned people to act as internal and external influencers. Participants should be willing to interact with your brand if your design is appealing. Your design must be long-term optimized and build strong user involvement.

According to David Kleinman, Managing Director of Giantstep, a creative tech firm, the majority of the effort of Giantstep now in the metaverse is for SM Entertainment, one of Korea's top entertainment firms, that represents many top K-Pop musicians. Everything is connected to a metaverse, from digital characters and avatars to the world's first ticketed virtual concert event, a full-fledged web series, and even merchandise.

For a typical business with a plethora of products and innumerable consumer touchpoints, there is no predicting how broad this can be." We may discuss how design, storytelling, and real-time technologies can be combined to build the future metaverse. Whatever the business, the goal is to infuse brand loyalty through physical-world AND virtual engagements."

According to Panchenko, any firm should begin by building a virtual version of their product – virtual products. Individuals prefer virtual products to real ones when it comes to getting closer to businesses. According to a Wired article, the market of the virtual product, which is the largest bridge between the physical and virtual environments, is currently valued at $50 billion and will continue to grow significantly in the coming years.

Brands' Future in the Metaverse

Today's businesses are largely digital-first. Some people establish their brand on the internet before launching a physical product. They can put these abilities to use in the metaverse. They can continue to develop digital personalities and content, as well as grow into virtually connected products. In the metaverse, those who know internet culture, digital art, and gaming activities will flourish.

Now is the time for brands to seize the opportunity and embrace the digital future. Businesses may use their experience with the internet and social media to stay ahead of the competition in the new virtual world. The metaverse may appear to be yet another big thing as part of digital transformation. Instead, see the metaverse as a way to broaden your businesses' reach, what they do, and how they do it.

CONCLUSION

Suppose you are still trying to wrap your brain around virtual reality, augmented reality, mixed or extended reality ideas. In that case, it is time to move on because more tech firms are talking about a new era of the internet known as the metaverse.

Despite its ambiguous definition, the word "metaverse" is commonly used to express the idea of a future iteration of the internet consisting of shared, 3D virtual places linked into an imagined virtual world. In basic terms, the metaverse is a virtual environment where you may use avatars to interact with other individuals in different geographical locations. Tech firms are considering various sorts of metaverse platforms. Users will be able to buy land and develop ecosystems using NFTs and cryptocurrencies on a blockchain-based platform. A robust virtual environment where individuals may work, play, or interact could be another sort of platform. However, creating a metaverse will rely heavily on AI and machine learning, as the metaverse's goal will be to combine our physical world with the virtual space via avatars. The metaverse will be the convergence of virtual reality and augmented reality.

The development of the metaverse will affect every facet of our civilization, especially entertainment, advertising, and the economy. The metaverse, however, will have legal ramifications. Collaboration and interoperability between metaverse developers will be one concern. Intellectual property rights will be another issue, which is the case with the most virtual product.

Even if the metaverse currently falls short of the long-term vision that many have for it, it has the potential to alter how we interact with the virtual environment dramatically. A collaborative virtual experience, similar to NFTs, might open up new options for creators, gamers, entrepreneurs, investors, tech firms, and artists, not only restructuring but inventing the digital economy.

The metaverse's virtual environment has the potential to become a trillion-dollar enterprise. It is a go-to spot for entertainment, shopping, and, for some, even jobs. The metaverse is being referred to as a successor of the internet rather than an extension of it.

AOA

- meta-verse: studio
  livestreams
  break out space

juke box
w/ coins: pay to choose songs

pay premium to
keep playlist in order
or first come first serve

Alicia?

NFT releases — invest in
AOA tracks?

→ invest in future
releases?

→

tokens ⇒ experiences ⇒ community
crowd source support + payment
in tokens; in-verse assets?

RF - where to sell?

- Sandbox
- Decentraland
- opensea
- Roblox?
- Minecraft?

Made in the USA
Middletown, DE
19 January 2022